FOCUS ON EDUCATION

Series Editor: Trevor Kerry

Teaching Mathematics

A teaching skills workbook

Keith Selkirk M.A.

Lecturer in Education

Macmillan Education

London and Basingstoke

First published 1984

Published by
MACMILLAN EDUCATION LIMITED
Houndmills Basingstoke Hampshire RG21 2XS
and London
Associated companies throughout the world

Printed in Hong Kong

ACKNOWLEDGEMENTS

The format of this book was developed by bringing together ideas used in a Post Graduate Certificate in Education course in mathematics teaching method, and the style of writing which has been adopted by the Teacher Education Project. The mathematics method course was initiated by Michael Barber, David Hale and myself and has been developed by Michael and me in conjunction with several other lecturers. We have worked so closely together that it would be difficult to say who originated many of the ideas; to all I am grateful. In draft form the book has been used with students by Susan Pirie and Malcolm Swan as well as by Michael and me; and to them as well as to our students, I owe thanks for much constructive criticism. A number of my former students have offered helpful suggestions from the standpoint of more mature teachers. I am also grateful to Keith Gardner for suggesting Activity 9.

While the book derives in style from the earlier productions of the Teacher Education Project, I have tried to avoid direct plagiarism. In a few cases, however, I have adapted tasks from other books in the series where I have felt the ideas were particularly valuable. I must thank Ted Wragg and Trevor Kerry for supporting the idea of a curriculum series, especially Trevor for his continued belief in it and his persistence in getting it off the ground, and also his wife Carolle for much dogged behind-the-scenes assistance in producing the series. Thanks are also due to the typists who have helped to produce the various drafts, especially Phyll Morris and Paula Hill.

Throughout the preparation of this book I have been fully aware of the books produced by the Mathematics Teacher Education Project (which has no direct connection with this project) edited by G.T. Wain and Derek Woodrow and published by Blackie. This book is in no way intended to compete with these books (which I recommend) but rather to supplement them by offering a new approach to a rather different aspect of teacher training.

CONTENTS

Editor's Preface   4

Introduction   5

PART 1 PREPARING TO TEACH MATHEMATICS

Activity 1   Background reading   7

Activity 2   Blackboard and overhead projector   8

Activity 3   Investigations   11

Activity 4   Lesson observation   13

Activity 5   New mathematical content   15

Activity 6   Planning lessons   16

Activity 7   Lesson organisation and control   18

Activity 8   Marking   20

Activity 9   Comprehending textbooks   22

Activity 10   Individual pupil behaviour   24

Activity 11   Puzzles and games   26

Activity 12   Teaching practice school   27

PART 2 TEACHING MATHEMATICS

Focus 1   Learning names   31

Focus 2   Resources survey   32

Focus 3   Writing worksheets   34

Focus 4   Handling difficult classes   39

Focus 5   Oral questioning   43

Focus 6   Investigations   46

Focus 7   Keeping pupil records   48

Focus 8   Exceptional pupils   52

PART 3 REFLECTIONS ON EXPERIENCE

Activity 13   Taking stock   56

Activity 14   The method project   58

Activity 15   Assessment of pupils' work   60

Activity 16   Medium-term planning   63

Activity 17   Goals in mathematics teaching   65

The Probationary Year: A Postscript for Student Teachers   69

Professionalism: A Final Thought   71

Further Reading   72

EDITOR'S PREFACE

The titles in this series are designed to examine basic teaching skills in their respective subject areas. Each title is laid out as a workbook so that the practitioner can utilise his or her own classroom as a basis for progressive professional self-development.

Impetus for the series came out of the DES-financed Teacher Education Project, which ran from 1976 to 1980 in the Universities of Nottingham, Leicester and Exeter. That project explored general teaching skills: class management, questioning, explaining and the handling of mixed ability classes and exceptional pupils. A direct outcome from the work of the Teacher Education Project was a series of skills' workbooks under the general title *Focus*, which was published by Macmillan during the years 1981 and 1982.

It is, perhaps, a measure of the success of the *Focus* series that I was approached by a number of colleagues in the involved universities with the proposal for a 'curriculum' series of workbooks which would apply some of the teaching skills highlighted and researched by the project to specific subject areas.

Each title in the current curriculum series is aimed at subject teachers in the appropriate field. Our corporate intention is to make each workbook immediately relevant to the needs of three main groups of users: qualified teachers of the subject in question; teachers qualified in some other discipline who find themselves pressed into service on less familiar ground; and students in training in the subject area concerned. Past experience has led us to believe that each exercise is adaptable for use at various levels of sophistication according to the stage reached by the user and to his or her own needs.

Each workbook has a tripartite format. Part 1 is intended to start the user thinking about issues in the particular curriculum area, and the activities designed for this purpose can often be carried out away from the classroom itself. In Part 2 a collection of practical exercises encourages teachers to become more self-aware and to scrutinise their own practice. Part 3 helps the teachers reflect on practice and experience by relating classroom events to research and theory. Within this basic structure individual authors are given some flexibility to interpret their own theme.

The series makes frequent demands on teachers to get together in order to watch one another at work: a process we have labelled 'observational pairing'. Traditionally the classroom has been 'a fine and private place' as Marvell might have put it. We believe that professional self-respect demands that a more open attitude should prevail.

It is especially opportune to be producing the curriculum series of workbooks at a time when economic stringencies are making in-roads into the education service in general and into in-service provision in particular. There is mounting public pressure for increased accountability by the teaching profession. This series will, we believe, help to make teachers more analytical in their teaching and more articulate in expressing the rationale for their work. It will also fill a void for really practical advice for all those whose jobs involve a responsibility for professional training, as university and college tutors, inspectors, advisers, teachers' centre wardens, headteachers, and heads of subject departments.

Dr Trevor Kerry
University of Nottingham

INTRODUCTION

This book was originally designed for a Post Graduate Certificate in Education course, but one happy result of writing it has been that it is being found useful by serving teachers as well as by those on pre-service training. Many of the ideas in it need little or no adaptation to be used as a self-help device to refresh teaching techniques and develop the various skills needed in the classroom. Resources for in-service training are hard to come by, and at the same time teachers are now more aware that training should be an on-going activity throughout a teaching career. Heads of department are becoming more responsible for this work in schools, and this book recommends a number of helpful ideas to improve the effectiveness of their department's work. The many non-specialist teachers of mathematics in our schools should also find this workbook a very practical source of guidance.

Teaching involves a wide variety of skills and the Teacher Education Project has produced a series of books which concentrate on particular teaching skills. In this book these varied skills are placed specifically in a mathematical context, and in addition some attempt is made to strike a balance between the different skills which a teacher requires. This should be borne in mind as you work through the tasks. Some of these tasks you will enjoy doing, and tackle with enthusiasm; others you will find difficult; and some may seem unattractive to you. Perhaps it is these latter tasks which you should concentrate on; most of us try to avoid doing those things we are not good at, and often try to explain our poor performance by assuming that such tasks are unimportant.

The remaining remarks apply chiefly to those on pre-service courses of teacher training but others, too, would do well to remind themselves of the sentiments expressed here. *You will be teaching both mathematics and children.* A primary aim of this booklet is to bring together these two objects of the verb 'to teach'. Because many readers will have a mathematical degree or other specialist qualification, we shall concentrate only on those aspects of mathematics which will impinge directly on your teaching. Student readers may have had little experience of children of secondary school age since leaving school as pupils; thus some of the tasks relevant to the children you will be teaching are located towards the end of the book, when you will have had some practical experience of schools and children.

As a teacher in the classroom you will probably feel very vulnerable and isolated. This places a great responsibility on you to prepare your work and to perform your job well. One of the objectives of this booklet is to encourage you to be self-critical of your work, and criticism can be both favourable and unfavourable. Good teachers are never satisfied with their performance and the best retain their habits of self-criticism to the ends of their careers. For this reason, many of the tasks are worth repeating at intervals throughout your career as part of an on-going effort at self-improvement. It is precisely for this purpose that a serving teacher will turn to a practical workbook such as this.

The sections of this workbook are arranged in a pattern which is common in many PGCE initial training courses. However, PGCE, B.Ed and INSET activities vary so widely that most users, especially practising teachers, will have to modify the structure to suit their specific purposes.

Part 1 PREPARING TO TEACH MATHEMATICS

Effective teaching depends upon sound preparation. For this reason Part 1 of this workbook examines a range of preparation skills in mathematics teaching. An outline of the tasks or activities you should attempt in order to acquire the habit of good preparation is given in the following table. Student users may find it most valuable to tackle the activities sequentially; more experienced teachers may wish to be selective. Even for the latter it is a good idea to begin by reviewing current practices in teaching in a systematic way; as with driving a car, it is easy to slip into unhelpful habits.

Activity	Title	When to do it (for PGCE students)	Date completed
1	Background reading	Week 1	
2	(a) Blackboard	Week 1 or 2	
	(b) Overhead projector	Week 1 or 2	
3	Investigations	Weeks 2-6	
4	Lesson observation	School visit 1	
5	New mathematical content	Weeks 3-7	
6	Planning lessons	Before school visit 2	
7	Lesson organisation and control	School visit 3	
8	Marking	School visits 3-5	
9	Comprehending textbooks	Week 5	
10	Individual pupil behaviour	School visit 5	
11	Puzzles and games	Weeks 6-8	
12	Teaching practice school	Weeks 7 or 8	

**Activity 1
BACKGROUND
READING**

Aims: 1 To alert you to the vast amount of reading, much of it enjoyable, which is relevant to mathematics teaching.

2 To encourage you to find your way about the library.

When to do this: Week 1

Time to spend: An hour, plus the time you spend reading what you find.

What to do: Browse in the library among the books on mathematics and education. Avoid both school and higher level text books. You should find plenty of suitable books; some may be in the mathematics section, others in the mathematical education section. If you have a mathematics method room you will probably find suitable books there, but look in the libraries as well. Make a list of such books; six are given below to start you off.

Author	Title	Publisher	Date	Library Reference
Fletcher, T.J. (Ed.)	*Some Lessons in Mathematics*	C.U.P.	1964	
Sawyer, W.W.	*Mathematician's Delight*	Penguin	1943	
Hunter, J. and Cundy, M.	*The Mathematics Curriculum: Number*	Blackie	1978	
Holt, M. and Marjoram, D.T.E.	*Mathematics in a Changing World*	Heinemann	1973	
Gardner, M.	*New Mathematical Diversions*	Allen & Unwin	1966	
Skemp, R.	*The Psychology of Mathematics*	Penguin	1971	

Follow up

(i) Students will find it useful to continue this list through the year in the mathematics method file. An even better idea is to start a card index with brief notes and keep it *throughout your teaching career*. Some of the books you note may be useful in completing future tasks.

(ii) Obtain a copy of *Booklists for the Teaching of Mathematics in Schools* from the Mathematical Association. This was first published in 1980, and is kept on computer file so that it can be continually up-dated.

(iii) Find out where the back numbers of journals for mathematics teachers are kept, particularly *Mathematics Teaching* and *Mathematics in School*, and browse through some of the recent issues.

(iv) Start reading.

**Activity 2
BLACKBOARD AND
OVERHEAD
PROJECTOR**

Aims: To practise two skills which you will use throughout your teaching career:
1 Use of blackboard (or whiteboard)
2 Use of overhead projector (OHP)

When to do this: Week 1 or 2

Time to spend: 2 × half an hour.

What to do: Effective teaching benefits greatly from the acquisition of certain skills. Trouble can be saved if these are practised beforehand outside the stress of the actual teaching situation. Here we practise two basic communication skills.

(a) Blackboard

Find an empty room with a blackboard. (Some schools are now using whiteboards with water-based pens and you may try this exercise with a whiteboard as well as, or instead of, a blackboard if you wish.) Clean the board and write the following:

Simultaneous equations   *Date*
A firm of contractors has two types of truck. When 4 of the first type and 1 of the second are used, the total load is 52 tons. When 2 of the first and 5 of the second are used, the total load is 80 tons. What loads can be carried by each type of truck?

Go and sit at the back of the room (this is important) and admire your work. Answer the questions below (the final columns are for the second part of this focus).

	BLACKBOARD	OHP
1 Did you start off with the background really clean?		
2 Can you read your writing? Honestly?		
3 Is your writing too big, too small, or just right?		
4 Is your writing too thick, too thin or just right?		
5 Are the shapes of any of your letters not clear?		
6 Is your writing horizontal?		
7 Is your writing even in size?		
8 Is your punctuation clearly visible?		

Now solve the problem on the board by an algebraic method.

Be particularly careful to distinguish the letter 'x' from the multiplication symbol ×; it is best to write the letter in manuscript thus: x. Make sure that you can distinguish '2's and 'Z's, '5's and 'S's and that decimal points are clearly visible. Go to the back of the room and answer the following questions.

	BLACKBOARD	OHP
1 Is your solution neatly spaced?		
2 Did you define your unknown quantities clearly?		
3 Are all numbers, letters and symbols unambiguous?		
4 Are your equality symbols neatly under one another?		
5 Are equation pairs bracketed?		
6 Does each step begin with a suitable symbol ($\therefore$, $\Rightarrow$ or $\Longleftrightarrow$)?		
7 Did you include a check of your solution?		
8 Did you jump any elementary steps in your solution?		

Return to the board again and solve the problem by using a graphical method. Make use of several colours. If a squared board is available, you might like to try this task with and without using the squared board.

From the back of the room answer the following questions.

	BLACKBOARD	OHP
1 Which colours show up best?		
2 Which colours show up badly?		
3 Are your straight lines straight?		
4 Would a ruler have helped?		
5 Did you label origin, axes and scale on the graph?		
6 Is the solution reasonably accurate?		
7 Is the solution convincing?		
8 Did you try to get away with just drawing the graph and omitting the rest of the solution?		

Unless you are inordinately proud of your work, clean the board.

(b) Overhead Projector

You may be less familiar with the overhead projector than with the blackboard. It has the disadvantage that it is more costly and fragile (and therefore fallible) than the blackboard, but it has many advantages. The two most obvious are:

(i) work can be prepared in advance on separate sheets of acetate and stored easily for repeated use.
(ii) you do not need to turn your back on the class while you are writing.

In this activity we shall concentrate on the OHP as a replacement for the blackboard. Using either the problem given above, or preferably another one, find an empty room with an OHP and repeat the task given above for the blackboard. Bear the following points in mind while you are performing this task:

(i) Use OHP pens with water-based ink if possible so that the acetate roll can be wiped clean with a damp cloth.
(ii) Make sure the OHP image fills the screen, is in focus, and is as little distorted in shape as possible by the angle of projection.
(iii) Do not draw the curtains or blinds.
(iv) While writing try to stand so that your body does not hide the beam of light to the screen.
(v) Avoid the temptation to look at the screen; once it is adjusted you can see how well your work looks on the OHP table itself.
(vi) When you have finished do not turn the electricity off immediately; turn the light off but leave the fan running for a time to cool the bulb.
(vii) Avoid moving the OHP while the bulb is warm.
(viii) Clean the acetate roll after use if you can.

Compare the advantages and disadvantages of the two aids with one or more fellow students and list your points.

BLACKBOARD	OHP
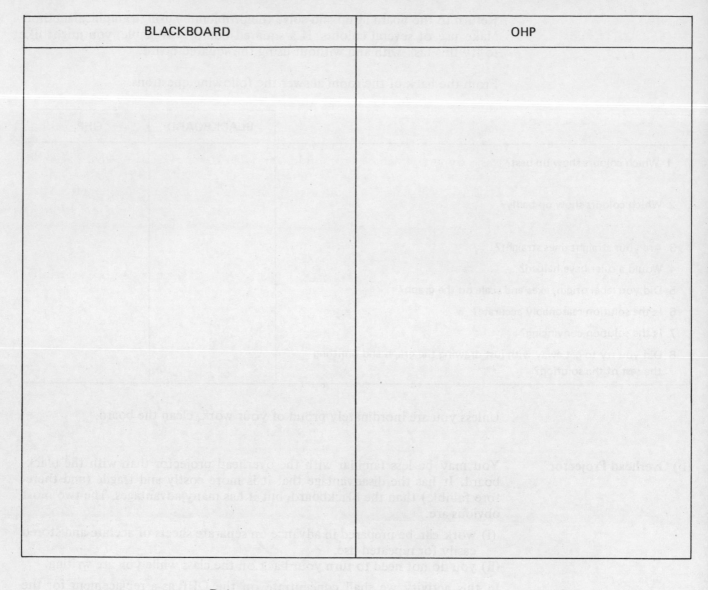

Points to remember

1 When teaching always carry chalk (or pens) and cleaning materials with you. A favourite game in many schools is hiding the blackboard duster.

2 Your own standards of neatness should provide an example for your pupils. Neatness will encourage more accurate working and make pupils' work easier to mark.

3 Pedantry in minor details is often necessary to drive home important mathematical points.

4 Blackboard and OHP may legitimately be used as 'jotters' to emphasise points you wish to make. While not all work will need to be set out in meticulous detail, some of your solutions should be presented in finished form.

Follow-up

(i) Get into the habit of looking at your blackboard and OHP work from the back of the room from time to time while you are teaching, and assessing it.

(ii) Always read through what you have written on the blackboard or OHP and check it for errors which might cause pupil misunderstandings.

(iii) After teaching practice rewrite and extend your comparison of the advantages and disadvantages of blackboard and OHP.

**Activity 3
INVESTIGATIONS**

Aims: 1 To develop the creative side of your mathematical ability.
2 To suggest teaching ideas which will help children to develop similar abilities.

When to do this: Weeks 2-6.

Time to spend: Four hours plus the time you spend thinking about it.

What to do: Some readers will have done similar tasks in undergraduate courses either in applied mathematics or in mathematical education courses. Take some simple situation understandable to an average 13-year-old child, and develop your own mathematics from it. Do not aim particularly at mathematical depth, but at insight into the underlying mathematical processes involved.

The intention is to develop mathematics as a creative, open-ended and original subject where one cannot always look at the back of the book for the answer. Even for mathematics graduates, this idea is sometimes startling. Some suitable topics are:

1 The Fibonacci sequence
2 The layout of numbers round a dartboard
3 Think of a number, halve it if it is even, treble it and add one if it is odd. What sequences do you obtain?
4 Patterns of hexagons on paper covered with a triangular pattern of dots
5 The game of nim where two players remove any number up to a given maximum of matches from a pile. The player to take the last match wins (or loses).
6 The patterns of shapes made from joining six equilateral triangles edgewise in a plane.

Many more ideas can be found in:

Banwell, C.S., Saunders, K.D. and Tahta, R., *Starting Points*, London, Oxford University Press, 1972.
Hardy, T., Howarth, A., Love, E. and McIntosh, A., *Points of Departure — 1 and 2*, Derby, Association of Teachers of Mathematics, no date.
Watson, F.R., *A Handbook of Number Investigations*, Leicester, Mathematical Association, 1981.

Back numbers of *Mathematics Teaching* and *Mathematics in School* will suggest more ideas, *Mathematical Gazette* may also give you more advanced investigations to try. Your own ideas, however, may well be even better since you have a personal stake in them, but if you are a PGCE or B.Ed student you ought to discuss your chosen investigation with your tutor before making a final decision. An example of an investigation plan might be:

Title: Layout of numbers round a dartboard.
Lines of investigation:
1 Are the numbers evenly balanced?
  (a) How might a better balance be obtained?
  (b) Measurement of imbalances. Vectors?
2 Are differences between adjacent numbers as large as possible?
  (a) Crude differences
  (b) Squares of differences.
Possible classroom benefits:
Practice in simple arithmetic
Development into some simple statistical ideas
Sequences
Random Numbers

11

Now write down your planned investigation.

Title:

Lines of investigation:

Possible classroom benefits:

Work at your investigation over the next few weeks from time to time, concentrating on your own development of the ideas in it rather than on classroom uses. Do not worry if it does not go exactly according to plan as you work at it; some avenues will seem unproductive, while other ones will open up. The end result may bear only a limited resemblance to your original intention. Try to generalise any results you obtain, but do not be afraid to investigate particular cases either, or to broaden or narrow your approach as seems necessary.

If you are a PGCE or B.Ed student your investigation can be written up as part of your mathematics method file, and your tutor will probably wish to see it and discuss it with you at intervals. When you have written up your investigation, describe briefly as a final section how you might use the idea in the classroom for an extended piece of pupil work over several periods, stating the ages and abilities of those for whom you think it would be suitable.

Follow-up

(i) Try investigating suitable mathematical situations yourself from time to time.

(ii) Next term you should, if possible, try out your investigation with a class in years 1-3 over several periods; see Focus 6.

**Activity 4
LESSON OBSERVATION**

Aim: To help you to observe how an experienced teacher (maybe a colleague) organises a lesson and handles the pupils.

When to do this: On your first school visit.

Time to spend: Two lessons, and half an hour soon afterwards.

What to do: It is assumed for student teachers that each week for five weeks you will be visiting a school for a half or whole day. During this time you will work as one of a pair with a fellow-student, gradually taking over responsibility for the lessons from the class teachers. On this first visit you will be spending most of your time observing, or working with individual pupils. Observing teaching can be boring, so this activity is designed to show you what to look for.

During the lessons make short rough notes below about what happens under the various headings. Under some headings, you may, of course, have nothing to write. At this stage you should concentrate on describing what happens rather than making a critical appraisal. If you have difficulty in deciding what to write, Activity 7 and Focus 5 may offer some ideas.

More experienced teachers rarely have a chance to view colleagues in action. To do so can be a valuable experience. This activity should help you, too, to observe the process of teaching with more analytical eyes.

	LESSON 1 class: ability level:	LESSON 2 class: ability level:
1 Lesson beginning		
2 Transitions from one activity to another		
3 Lesson ending		
4 Explanations and instructions		
5 Questioning		
6 Whole class teaching		
7 Group work		
8 Individual work		

At some times in the lesson the teacher will probably be talking to individuals or groups. At these times try to listen carefully, but unobtrusively, to the way the teacher handles the problems of communication in these situations. Write up your notes briefly afterwards under the headings below.

	LESSON 1	LESSON 2
1 Language level of teacher		
2 Non-verbal interactions between teacher and pupils		
3 Variety of approach		
4 Apportionment of teacher's time		
5 Appropriateness of content and materials		

Make arrangements to teach at least one of the classes on your next visit (see Activity 6).

Follow-up

(i) Compare your notes with those of the fellow-student (or with a fellow-teacher) who sat in on the lesson with you.

(ii) Students can also compare and discuss notes with those of students who sat in on other lessons.

(iii) If possible discuss the lessons with the teacher concerned, probing particularly the decisions made by the teacher before and during the lesson.

**Activity 5
NEW MATHEMATICAL
CONTENT**

Aims: 1 To help you to cover content areas of school mathematics where your own knowledge is weak.
2 To accustom you to a careful reading of school mathematics texts.
3 To help you to keep up your own interest in and enjoyment of mathematics.

When to do this: At intervals during Weeks 3-7.

Time to spend: At least five hours.

What to do: All mathematics teachers have weak areas in their mathematical knowledge, even newly qualified mathematics graduates. In some areas you might be almost ashamed to admit ignorance; but some areas you might never had had the opportunity to study.

Examples of areas you might not have studied are:

1 Kinematics
2 Newtonian mechanics
3 Flow charts
4 Programming in BASIC (or some other language)
5 Descriptive statistics
6 Inferential statistics
7 Transformation geometry
8 Euclidean geometry
9 Applications of maths to electricity
10 Surveying
11 Navigation
12 Numerical analysis
13 Aspects of matrices
14 Latitude and longitude
15 Probability

In this Activity concentrate on the mathematics, not on teaching it. This means that most graduates will want to look at topics at the sixth form level rather than at main-school level; non-specialist teachers may have 'blank spots'. Some readers may wish to study sections of an examination syllabus which are unfamiliar to them. Choose a suitable topic (either part or all of one of the topics mentioned above or a different one) and if you are a student obtain your method tutor's approval of it. Find two or three school texts which cover your chosen topic and work carefully through one of them. Do not try too much unless you really feel the need; about three chapters of an A-level text will be sufficient. Solve enough exercises to make sure you understand the principles involved and to feel you could tackle the teaching of the topic to a suitable group of pupils. Use the alternative texts for supplementary material and compare the different approaches and levels of difficulty. If you are a student you should discuss your work with your mathematics method tutor on completion; but everyone should keep their notes and solutions carefully filed for future use.

Subject:

	Author	Title	Chapters
Main text:			
Additional texts:			

Follow-up

You will need to repeat this task *throughout your teaching career*. It is important to make sure you have a good grasp of the topics you need to teach before you try to teach them, but it is just as valuable to sustain a lively interest by extending the bounds of your own knowledge of mathematics whenever the opportunity arises.

Aim: To help you to plan your teaching effectively. This task concentrates on the framework of the lesson plan. The actual content of the planned lesson is one of the major considerations of any teaching course, so important that there is not space to tackle it in detail in a book this size. Fletcher (quoted in Activity 1) has some good ideas, and Brissenden (see Follow-up) gives further help in this area.

When to do this: For students during school visit 2; and for every subsequent lesson you teach. Experienced teachers will need to engineer appropriate opportunities.

Time to spend: Too much.

What to do: If you are a student you should try to arrange to teach at least one of the classes you saw on visit 1, though the class teacher will probably wish to be present as well as the fellow student who is working with you. You will find it helpful to discuss your lessons with this student before and after teaching them and you may wish to teach jointly.

Every lesson you teach must be planned, even teachers who search hurriedly for a suitable exercise in the textbook as the pupils enter the room are planning their lessons. But you must do a lot better than this (except in emergencies). Keep your lesson notes carefully in a mathematics lesson file and discuss them from time to time with your tutor, if you are a student. More experienced teachers should occasionally discuss them with colleagues.

Lesson Notes. Whenever you plan a lesson you will have to write notes, both for reference and to clarify your own thinking. They should be long enough to give you a good guide about what you want to do in the lesson (and possibly to use again next year if the lesson is a success) and short enough for you to refresh your memory from, while keeping one eye on the class. A page of A4 is usually enough, though some lessons may only need the odd line or two, and others, particularly with the sixth form, will require extended notes.

Most tutors of students are simply happy to see that your lesson notes exist; the proof of the pudding is after all in the actual lessons you teach, and they will only become critical if your lessons are not successful. However, all lesson notes should have the following points made clear:

1 *Title*
   When and to whom the lesson is to be taught, and a rough idea of the contents.

2 *Aims*
   These can be covered by the title, but it is a mistake to get into the habit of doing this; aims will usually, if not always, need to be amplified more carefully. *Aims should not be solely mathematical*: there are at least three other types of aim. These are (with examples):
   (a) Management: to learn names, to try to keep control, to improve distribution and collection of materials.
   (b) Teaching method: to try out videotapes, to develop group work, to develop your questioning skills.
   (c) Social: to encourage co-operation rather than competition, to involve disinterested pupils, to encourage a happier working atmosphere.

3 *The plan itself*
   This is where your imagination comes into play. You might find the following points useful in planning:

(a) It is often helpful to plan a lesson in clear stages and make a note of your intended timing. You can compare this with the actual timing in the lesson if you are not too busy, and this will gradually help you to learn one of the most difficult problems of planning, just how much to put in each lesson.

(b) Do not talk too much. Pupils mostly learn mathematics by doing it, not by listening to you. Your difficulty will probably be to stop talking rather than knowing what to say.

(c) Concentrate on beginnings, transitions and endings. These are always the danger points for classroom control, so think about how you are going to manage them (see Activity 7).

(d) Many lessons will only need brief notes because you or other teachers have prepared worksheets or cards, or because for much of the lesson your class will be doing exercises. Remember to work through these beforehand, and whenever possible try to bring the class together for a few minutes at the beginning and end of the lesson.

(e) Prepare a set of full solutions or a list of answers to any exercises. This is invaluable for saving time in the lesson, and may help you to begin marking pupils' work in the class.

(f) You may want to write and duplicate your own worksheets. If so, this is a good opportunity to find out how to do this, especially to use the ubiquitous spirit duplicator. Remember not to leave the task of duplicating until the last minute.

(g) Don't be too ambitious at first.

(h) Lesson notes should be your servant, not your master. Students should not need to copy them up in their best handwriting (though they should, of course, be legible). You should also be prepared occasionally to throw them out of the window (metaphorically) while you are teaching.

4 *Resource list*

Always list the resources you require for the lesson, this can be a great help on a busy teaching day. Make sure well in advance that the resources will be available when you want them; if you plan the lesson too late, they may not be available.

5 *Critique*

This is important and should not be skimped. For students your tutor will probably use it so that he or she can place your work in perspective, and will possibly discuss the points you make; but do not let this inhibit what you say, the chief reason for writing the critique is to develop your own personal analysis of your teaching. When writing the critique try to strike a balance between class and individual problems (both of mathematics and discipline) and your own faults of planning and execution.

Follow-up

(i) Never neglect lesson planning.

(ii) After each lesson make sure you write up the critique as soon as you have time; it is surprising how quickly you will forget the points you wished to make. Even very experienced teachers will benefit from this analytical approach; and time spent on self-appraisal is never wasted.

(iii) You will find further help in this area from Brissenden, T.H.F., *Mathematics Teaching: Theory and Practice*, London, Harper and Row, 1980.

Activity 7
LESSON ORGANISATION AND CONTROL

Aim: To help to start developing your own classroom organisation and control.

When to do this: For students, on your third school visit; teachers will make their own opportunities.

Time to spend: One lesson, and half an hour soon afterwards.

What to do: This is a follow-up to Activities 4 and 6. Pick one of the lessons you will be taking and plan it carefully, paying particular attention to the points stressed below. If you can persuade a colleague to sit in on the lesson, or if you are a student working as one of a pair, so much the better. You will then be able to cross-check your impressions with those of an impartial observer, and can fill in the notes together.

Date: Class: Ability level:

1   *Lesson beginning*

    Were you there before the class?
    Were you able to start promptly?
    Was your start effective?
    Were all your materials available?
    Did you make the purpose of the lesson clear?

2   *Transitions between activities*
(These are the most difficult times from the point of view of classroom control.)

    Were your instructions clear?
    Was there unnecessary noise?
    Could you have improved the distribution and collection of materials?

3   *Lesson ending*

Were you ready for the bell?

Did you sum up the lesson?

Did you point the way ahead?

Did you give clear instructions about any homework?

Did you collect books and/or materials?

Did the pupils leave quietly?

Did you leave the room tidy?

4   *Misbehaviour*

Describe briefly a piece of misbehaviour (no matter how trivial)

What were the reasons for the misbehaviour? Boredom, not knowing what to do, high spirits, anti-social behaviour, or what?

What action did you take?

After discussion with your colleague (and for students, with the class teacher), describe how you would try to react if the same situation happened again.

Follow-up

(i) Pay particular attention to beginnings, transitions and endings of lessons.

(ii) Find out anything you can from regular teachers or tutors about the background of the pupils who misbehave. Do you feel more sympathetic towards them now?

(iii) Bear in mind the need to learn names (see Focus 1)

(iv) Repeat this task informally from time to time on your other school visits and on your main teaching practice.

(v) You will find further help in this area in: Wragg, E.C., *Class Management and Control*, Basingstoke, Macmillan Education, 1981.

**Activity 8
MARKING**

Aim: To initiate consideration of the importance of marking pupils' work.

When to do this: For students, school visits 3-5; or as appropriate over a span of three lessons.

Time to spend: Teaching time as appropriate. One-two hours' marking time.

What to do: 1 Arrange to set some homework based on at least one of your lessons. If you are a student you should discuss the amount with the class teacher.

2 Collect the work and afterwards mark it (see below).

3 Give the work back, going over difficult points and commenting as necessary.

Note: For students on weekly visits this arrangement is far from ideal because the whole process takes a fortnight and pupils will have forgotten what the work is about by the time you give it back. If you can possibly make arrangements to shorten this time to one week, then do so. Practising teachers will meet the class more often.

Marking has two main objectives. One is to correct the pupil's mistakes and the other to inform you of his or her progress. If you know your class well, the former will be the dominant objective. The actual giving of a numerical mark for every piece of work will be unnecessary (though, oddly, pupils often want marks), but you will need to make sure the pupils are appraised of their mistakes, so their work must be seen by you. The best time to do this is individually while they are with you in the class, but you will not be able to see all of everyone's work in class, and work should be seen at least once a week. Marking books can be tedious and is very time consuming, and you should not overdo it — your time may often be spent more fruitfully doing better preparation, or even watching TV or in the 'Pig and Whistle'. Sometimes children can mark their own or each other's work, but this is best left for drill exercises where corrections are easily seen. Beware of going over everything on the board; this wastes many pupils' time. You can speed up marking by efficient preparation. Routine exercises need a list of solutions for you to refer to. Problems will probably require working through in advance — it is embarrassing to give out an exercise you have not worked through and find it is far too easy or, worse still, far too difficult. Always keep a red ballpoint pen by you in class to fill in those odd moments marking pupils' work — it is amazing how much time you can save that way.

For this Activity students should not set too complicated an exercise. Work out solutions and decide on marks before starting your corrections, if possible with your fellow student. One problem of marking any exercise in mathematics is that of the balance of marks between having a correct method of solution and having an accurate solution. This can only be decided in the light of your objectives in setting the exercise. For many problem-type answers a good rule of thumb is to give half the marks for each. In any case there can be no marks for accuracy unless the method marks have been obtained. Another problem to be resolved is whether to follow through arithmetical inaccuracies early in the solution. This can be very time consuming and you must decide in each case whether it is worth the effort.

We shall return to further consideration of assessment in Activity 15. At this stage, discuss the work with your fellow student, the class teacher and, if possible, your tutor. Comment on what happened below:

Was the amount of homework about right?

Was it of the right difficulty? (All should have done some, some should have done all).

Did any pupil do an inadequate amount?

Did any pupil not hand in work? Did you take steps to find out the reasons for this?

Did every pupil do the right work and understand the instructions?

Did you have to amend your mark scheme in view of some of the solutions?

At this stage most students get very depressed about the time marking takes them. Think about how you could cut this down in future without skimping it.

Follow-up

Organise your marking schedule quickly at the beginning of your main teaching practice or contact with a class so that pupils see they will not get away with inadequate work. Keep careful check of those who do not hand in their books. A good ploy is to arrange to collect books in from each class on a different day so that you spread the load. Try to get a good proportion of your marking done in the actual lessons and in your free periods (students have more of these than the average teacher). Exercise books are heavy to carry home each evening, especially if you lack your own transport, and in any case you will need to spend time preparing lessons for the next day as well. Try never to get behind with marking — catching up with it is like a labour of Hercules.

21

**Activity 9
COMPREHENDING
TEXTBOOKS**

Aims: 1 To familiarise yourself with the detail of a school mathematical text.
2 To analyse its logic as a step towards understanding pupils' difficulties.

When to do this: Week 5 (approximately).

Time to spend: About half an hour on each section, plus group discussion time.

What to do: Mathematicians usually communicate through very brief statements. This means that texts must be read *very carefully indeed* since there are few redundant words, and care needs to be taken to ensure that what is written is understood. A simple way of doing this is to repeat the main points of a text in an original way. This is practicable because the majority of mathematical texts for children (apart from examples and exercises) is made up of either *instructions* or *explanations*. In both cases these proceed step by step. You should pick one passage of each type from a school text and proceed to complete the following tables.

1 **Instructions**

The example is based on *SMP Book D*, page 26, C.U.P.
Example: *Enlargement*

	Given	Action	Special cases	Result	Conclusion
1	Centre of enlargement, O, rectangle $ABCD$ and its enlargement $A'B'C'D'$ on same side of O.	Measure: OA and OA' OB and OB' etc.	O between A and A'; A' between O and A; O on $ABCD$	$OA'=2OA$ $OB'=2OB$ etc.	
2	–	Measure: AB and $A'B'$ BC and $B'C'$ etc.	–	$A'B'=2AB$ $B'C'=2BC$ etc.	Ratio of lengths on rectangles = ratio of distances from O

Topic: Source:

Given	Action	Special cases	Result	Conclusion

22

2 Explanations

The example is based on *SMP Book D*, pages 103-4, C.U.P.

Example: *Arrow Diagrams*

Situation	Conditions	Conclusions
1 Arrow diagram, set of people to set of drinks on given day	One person → many drinks Many people → one drink	MANY to MANY correspondence
2 Arrow diagram, same sets showing favourite drink	Many people → one drink Each person → one drink	MANY to ONE correspondence
3 Arrow diagram, same sets, each person has different drink, same number of drinks as people	Each person → one drink No person has same drink	ONE to ONE correspondence
4 Give example of ONE to MANY correspondence. (e.g. same set, to each drink give person most frequently drinking it).	Each drink from one person and one person only, maybe one person → many drinks, some people → no drinks	

Topic: Source:

Situation	Conditions	Conclusions

Follow-up

Draw up such diagrams as part of your preparation when teaching a new topic. They will help you to bring out the important points in the mathematics which you are about to teach.

Activity 10
**INDIVIDUAL PUPIL
BEHAVIOUR**

Aims: To concentrate your attention on the behaviour of individual pupils. (This is the third in the sequence of Activities 4, 7 and 10.)

When to do this: On your last school visit; or as appropriate.

Time to spend: One lesson, half an hour completing schedule, and group discussion.

What to do: Choose one child to watch in one of your colleague's lessons. For each minute enter what that child did on the schedule sheet on page 25. You may have up to three entries in any one minute. If there is only one entry, enter 1 against the activity; if there are two entries, enter ½ against each activity, and if there are three activities enter $^1/_3$ against each. If your lesson is longer than 35 minutes, stop after 35 minutes.

After the lesson, if you can, have a word with the pupil you have been making notes on without letting him or her know that you have done this. Note the responses below. Complete the totals and percentages on your schedule.

Your colleague should make a similar analysis in one of your lessons and you should enter the results on the sheet also for comparative purposes.

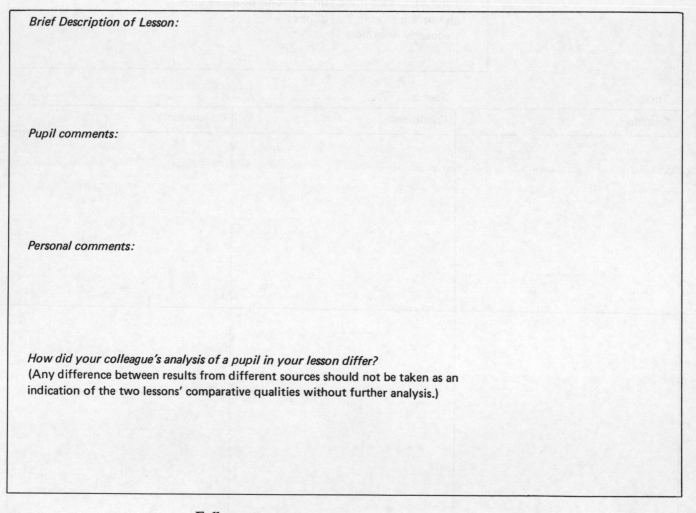

Brief Description of Lesson:

Pupil comments:

Personal comments:

How did your colleague's analysis of a pupil in your lesson differ?
(Any difference between results from different sources should not be taken as an indication of the two lessons' comparative qualities without further analysis.)

Follow-up

(i) Discuss the results of the analyses with your fellow-student, colleague or within the maths department.

(ii) If you are a student repeat the exercise with a more experienced teacher and compare the results with those previously obtained.

PUPIL OBSERVATION

CLASS: TITLE OF LESSON:

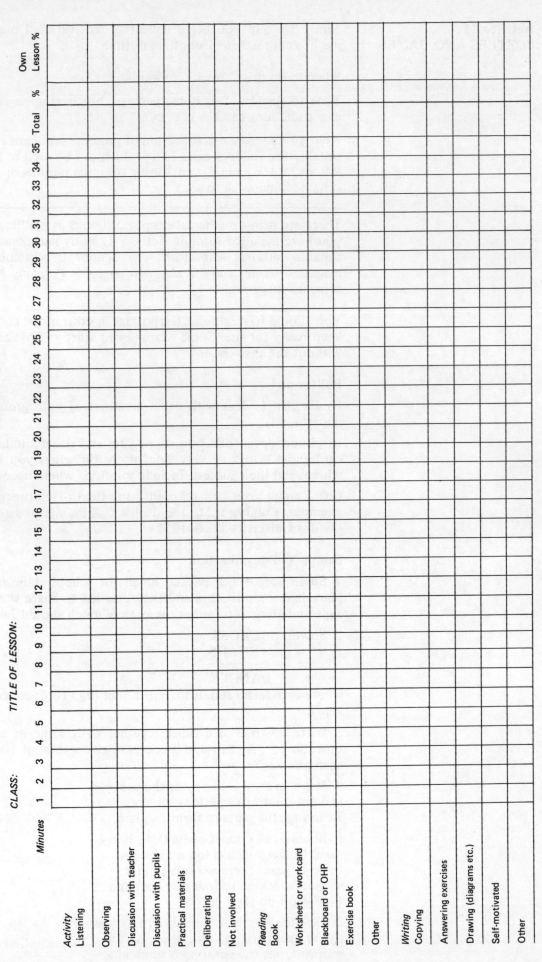

Minutes	1	2	3	4	5	6	7	8	9	10	11	12	13	14	15	16	17	18	19	20	21	22	23	24	25	26	27	28	29	30	31	32	33	34	35	Total	%	Own Lesson %
Activity																																						
Listening																																						
Observing																																						
Discussion with teacher																																						
Discussion with pupils																																						
Practical materials																																						
Deliberating																																						
Not involved																																						
Reading																																						
Book																																						
Worksheet or workcard																																						
Blackboard or OHP																																						
Exercise book																																						
Other																																						
Writing																																						
Copying																																						
Answering exercises																																						
Drawing (diagrams etc.)																																						
Self-motivated																																						
Other																																						

Aim: To help you begin collecting motivational materials which you can use in your teaching from time to time.

When to do this: Week 6 onwards.

Time to spend: Two hours perhaps, but *best done in odd moments* whenever something catches your eye.

What to do: Make a collection of puzzles, problems or mathematical games suitable for children aged 11-16 which can be used to fill in odd moments of lessons, at the end of term, during tutor set periods or when you do not have suitable homework to set.

There are many mathematical puzzle books available; you will probably find you have included some in Activity 1. Many magazines and newspapers have suitable puzzles; *Mathematics in School* is particularly useful, as is the magazine *Games and Puzzles*. *Mathematics Teaching* Nos. 84 and 87 suggest some useful games.

You should have at least ten puzzles in your initial collection which you can keep ready for use. Some examples to start you off are given below, though without the answers.

Follow-up

(i) Exchange ideas with other members of your group of students or your department.

(ii) Build up a collection of puzzles and other similar ideas (possibly on a card index), making very brief notes on when you have used them, with whom, and their success. Include solutions where necessary.

(iii) Extend your collection into the field of mathematical models (see, for example, Cundy, H.M. and Rollett, A.P., *Mathematical·Models*, London, Oxford University Press, 1951).

Sample puzzle collection

1 Susan forgot her packed lunch for school. Jane had 3 sandwiches and Mary had 5 sandwiches and they decided to share them equally. Susan paid Jane and Mary 24p for her share. How much should Jane and Mary receive?

2 Solve
        CROSS
      +ROADS
      ̄ ̄ ̄ ̄ ̄ ̄ ̄
       DANGER

where each letter stands for a different digit (0 does not necessarily stand for zero).

3 Write down 3 five times together with some or all of the arithmetical operations +, −, ×, ÷ and brackets to give a total of 100. Can you do it more than one way?

4 Make an accurate copy of the hexagon and cut it into five parts as shown. Rearrange the parts to form a square.

5 Boats A, B, C meet boats D, E, F in a canal tunnel which is too narrow for them to pass. There is a small wider section which will admit one boat at a time. How do they pass?

6 Find the length of the marked diagonal of the quadrilaterial. (No, there isn't a misprint, but the notation is unusual.)

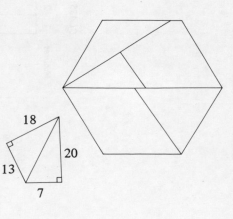

**Activity 12
TEACHING PRACTICE
SCHOOL**

Aim: This is for student use, to make sure you find out all relevant information about your teaching practice school.

Note: Experienced teachers may find this Activity useful as a guide for any less well-prepared students in their charge. Teachers in charge of students may care to read Trevor Kerry's *The New Teacher* in the *Focus* series, Macmillan Education, 1982.

When to do this: Week 7 or 8.

Time to spend: Half a day (or more if you are able).

What to do: You will probably have arrangements made for you to visit your main teaching practice school in advance. There is a lot to find out which will save trouble later, but try to avoid sounding like a market research interviewer. Dress fairly formally for your first visit, then take your cue from the staff. Begin by reporting to the school office: they will probably direct you to the staffroom. You should ask for your school tutor (who will usually be the Head of Mathematics), or for the teacher responsible for students. Remember that he or she will probably have lessons to teach, so you may feel rather unwanted. If you get the opportunity, go and help in the classroom, you will find out how the school works more quickly and in this way impress the staff by your keenness. The vital information which you should find out if possible is tabulated below and on the next two pages. Some schools will not have this available at once, they will want to meet you before making decisions. In this case you might have to go back to the school for a second visit.

Other points you may find useful are listed below; you might well find it easier to talk about some of them to younger members of staff who are not too beset with responsibilities.

1 If possible obtain lists of the classes you expect to teach and a mark book.

2 Ask about school rules and familiarise yourself with the punishments and sanctions which are in use. If possible obtain a list of the rules, and any booklet the school might produce for new members of staff.

3 Find out about the pastoral care system and if possible arrange to be attached to a class or registration group.

4 Discuss the school's attitude to homework.

5 Find out about any problem children you might expect in your classes.

6 Try to borrow copies of any text books/worksheets and other materials you may need; a copy of the mathematics department's timetable if one is available can also be useful.

7 Leave your name, address, and if possible telephone number with the person in charge of you and the school office so that they can contact you if necessary.

8 Discuss your visit with your University/College tutor afterwards.

Follow-up

(i) Prepare your mark book and first week's lessons.

(ii) Look through the tasks you will have to complete next term. *If you have sufficient time on your visit you will find it very helpful to start Focus 2 now* rather than leave it to next term.

Student's name:

Teaching practice school:

Postal address:

Telephone number:

Name of headmaster:

Teacher in charge of students (if any):

Name of school tutor:

Class/group attached to for registration:

First day of practice:

Last day of practice:

Half-term and other dates school is closed:

Dates of any special events
(e.g. swimming, galas, speech days, school trips):

Periods of examinations
(note classes involved):

Times of school day including breaks, lunch etc:

Other notes:

Finally: Make a copy of this and the following page for your University or College tutor and discuss any problems with him or her.

Timetable:

Lessons and times	Monday	Tuesday	Wednesday	Thursday	Friday
1					
2					
3					
4					
5					
6					
7					
8					

In each box enter the class and room number in which the lesson will take place. Note below the class teachers' names and the proposed syllabus, possibly including the approximate time to be spent on each section.

Class	Teacher	Syllabus

Part 2　　TEACHING MATHEMATICS

Note to students

By the end of your first term you will be itching to get into the classroom and do some 'real' teaching. You will, however, be worried about a number of the problems you are going to face; the following tasks highlight some of these and help to pinpoint potential difficulties. The tasks this term are related to your skills as a mathematics teacher and they do not assume you will have easy access to a library. For this reason they are labelled 'focus' rather than 'activity'. Because you are probably more worried about discipline and classroom management than other aspects of your teaching, the earlier tasks place more emphasis on this. By the second half of the term you should look more closely at some of the other skills you require.

One important task which you will have to perform throughout the term and which does not figure directly in the eight tasks below is that of lesson preparation. From time to time during the term you should look back at Activity 6 and refresh your memory about what it says. *All your lessons should be thoroughly prepared* in the way indicated there and your notes should be kept in your teaching practice file and seen regularly by your tutor.

Note to experienced teachers

The tasks which follow can be interpreted at a variety of levels to suit your own experience and circumstances. You will need to choose the order of the tasks according to opportunity. Where required, use the observational pairing technique with an interested colleague. The purpose of the eight Focuses is to encourage an analytical approach to the process of teaching. Since the classroom lesson is central to what teachers do, this part of the workbook is the pivot on which the rest hangs.

Focus	Title		When to do it (for PGCE students)	Date completed
1	Learning Names		Weeks 1-3	
2	Resources Survey		Week 1	
3	Writing Worksheets	A	Week 2	
		B	Week 3	
		C	Week 4	
4	Handling Difficult Classes	A	Week 4	
		B	Week 6	
5	Oral Questioning	A	Week 5	
		B	Week 7	
6	Investigations		Weeks 6-7	
7	Keeping Pupil Records		Week 7 onwards	
8	Exceptional Pupils		Weeks 8-10	

**Focus 1
LEARNING NAMES**

Aim: To focus your attention on the urgent need to learn pupils' names. Three of the most important skills in teaching are:
(a) Effective class management and discipline
(b) Questioning skills
(c) Development of personal relationships.
You will be able to learn these skills much more rapidly when you know your pupils' names.

When to do this: During the first three weeks of your teaching practice or whenever you take over a new class or set.

Time to spend: Odd moments in and out of class in the first three weeks of teaching contact with the pupils.

What to do: Rather than recommend one way of learning names, several suggestions are given which can be used separately or in any combination. One good idea is to try each method with a separate class and see which works best for you. Do not be tempted to let name learning go by the board, you will need to work hard at it, outside as well as inside the classroom.

Suggestion 1

This is a good way of learning names when every pupil has a fixed seat in the room. Simply draw up a rough plan of the classroom with every name in its place. This often works well but has the danger that you learn *places rather than faces*.

Suggestion 2

Try to learn three (no more) names per lesson and then write a brief one line description of the pupil after the lesson. Try to recall the names and faces at odd moments — in the bath, on the bus and so on. In each lesson use the names you already know as much as possible. If you find name-learning really hard this method can help if followed conscientiously.

Suggestion 3

With younger forms, make a game of it. Tell them you are going to do some work for a change and then try to name them round the class. Count two points if you get the name right and one if they have to give you a clue. See if you can beat your record. This needs a bit of self-confidence, and should not be attempted after the first week or two if the results are likely to be too shaming!

Some general points are worth emphasising:

1 Use names as much as you can at first as it is an essential first step (but only a first step) on the road to knowing your pupils well.

2 Give out and collect exercise books yourself until you know the pupils since this is a good opportunity to use their names. Later, pupils should do this task for you.

3 When you get more experience you will be able to use eye-contact instead of names. The danger for mature teachers is then that *eye-contact becomes a substitute for name-learning*.

4 Try to include as much oral questioning as you can in the early stages of getting to know a class. Have a blitz on mental arithmetic for example (see Focus 5). (For students this is easier said than done, for more experienced teachers it should become a habit.)

31

**Focus 2
RESOURCES SURVEY**

Aim: To help you to assess or re-assess the resources available to you in your school.

When to do this: For students, in the first week of your main teaching practice. If you spend enough time visiting your main teaching practice school in the previous term, then you should begin this survey then. Experienced teachers will make their own opportunities.

Time to spend: This depends on the resources available. Perhaps 1-2 hours unless you examine written materials in detail.

What to do: Make notes below on the various resources which are available to you as part of the mathematics department. The details to note will depend very much on the organisation of the department — if materials are widely scattered through the school, you should note where the items are kept; you might also wish to note if there are individual copies or class sets, if the materials are disposable, and if other teachers are likely to be using them.

How you use the resources will also depend on the mathematics department. In some schools you might have very little latitude and be expected to follow closely a scheme of work. This can be very comforting at first, but later on it can be frustrating if you have lots of ideas of your own, and might need some tactful negotiation. If you are involved in team teaching with one or more experienced teachers make sure that you do your share in the preparation and use of resources.

Textbooks

What books are your classes issued with? What other class sets are available for occasional use? Where are books with possible enrichment materials kept, and which have been found the most useful?

Worksheets and workcards

What commercially produced sets are available and how are they used?

What school-produced sets are available and how are they used? Are they disposable? If so, will you need to duplicate sets before using them? Will you be able to supplement them by producing additional or alternative materials? What are the objectives of the sheets: to allow pupils to work at their own speeds, to cater for above or below average pupils, as additional exercises, as information sheets, to initiate investigational work, etc?

What other disposable sheets are available; for example — patterned paper (dots, squares, graph grids, number tables etc.), duplicate examination papers and tests?

Reprographics

Has the school a reprographic unit? If so, how long does it take to produce copies of (i) handwritten worksheets, (ii) typed stencils, (iii) sheets with diagrams, etc. If not, has the school available for teacher use (i) photocopiers, (ii) heat copiers, (iii) spirit duplicators, (iv) typewriters: and are they available for students? Is there any restriction on the use of paper or stencils?

Classroom fixtures

Look at, and if necessary make a note about, the resources which are fixtures in rooms in which you will be teaching; for example, blackboards with squared patterns, whiteboards, screens for projectors and electric sockets. Note also any significant absence of resources, especially lack of suitable blackboards.

Visual and audio aids — for class use

What aids are available (OHP, slide projector, television, etc.)? What accompanying software is there (prepared acetate sheets and pens for OHP, film strips, video tapes, chalk and blackboard duster etc.)?

Aids for pupil use

What aids are available for pupil use? Are there sufficient for every member of the class, for a group, or only for one? Note geometrical instruments, rulers, pencils, dice, centicubes, geoboards, elastic bands etc. What materials are the pupils expected to provide (pens, pencils, rulers etc.)? What is the school policy about calculators?

Use of resources

Note here any interesting or original examples you see of other teachers in the school using the various resources above. (This section can be added to throughout your study period.)

Follow-up

(i) Check some suitable sheets or cards using Activity 9 and/or Focus 3.

(ii) Discuss with the colleagues concerned their aims in using the resources noted above.

(iii) Practise the use of any new or complicated equipment before using it in class.

(iv) Keep the resources list up to date, and make a note below of any further resources which you would have found useful during your teaching.

**Focus 3
WRITING WORKSHEETS**

Aim: To help you to set work for your pupils which is clearly written and of appropriate difficulty.

When to do this: Weeks 2-4.

Time to spend: One hour for each worksheet as part of your lesson preparation.

What to do: Writing effective worksheets demands that lessons should be prepared in good time since the sheets will have to be duplicated before the lesson. Too often this is done during morning assembly, and if the duplicator breaks down or someone else has got there first, there is not time to prepare alternative material. It is suggested that you write three worksheets specifically as part of this Activity, one in each of weeks 2, 3 and 4, but you will probably write many more during your teaching. (In some schools students might have to ask for approval for this Activity if your teaching context and method is laid down as part of the department's scheme.)

**Worksheet A: A Drill
Exercise (Week 2)**

Do not attempt too much with your first worksheet. A drill exercise of (say) twenty short questions will be a good start, especially if you have troubles with the mechanical process of using the duplicator. Pick a topic where the class needs some drill; for example, multiplication of fractions, solutions of linear equations without brackets, or areas of irregular polygons having all vertices right angled. Grade your examples carefully so that each new difficulty is encountered separately. Many old-fashioned textbooks such as those by Durell are particularly good at this. Check the answers (for example if an equation has a negative solution and the class has not done negative numbers you might cause problems). You may wish to set the sheet as classwork, as revision, as an assessment unit, as a test or as homework, but you should be sure about how you want to use it before writing it. Decide how much oral introduction you wish to give before the pupils start on the work (if any) and whether the answers will be made on your sheet or separately (the latter will enable the sheets to be used again). Consider the problems of giving out and collecting in the sheets.

Assessment

After you have marked the work, assess the pupils' reaction to it:

1 Were any of the questions too hard, so that only one or two pupils answered them correctly?

2 Were there enough easy questions for even the weakest pupils to have some success?

---

3 Did you allow too much or too little time for the pupils to do the work?

4 Did you arrange the questions in increasing order of difficulty (apart from intentional departures from this rule)?

5 If you used the sheet in class work, how much help did you have to give pupils (a) in explaining what to do, (b) in explaining how to do it?

6 Did you organise the distribution of the sheets and the collection of answers efficiently, using pupils to help if possible, or taking the opportunity to make sure you know everyone's name?

7 Was discipline easier or harder than normal with this class?

8 Is the worksheet worth keeping for future use?

Worksheet B: A Problem Exercise (Week 3)

This time you should attempt something a little more ambitious mathematically by asking, say, half a dozen problem-type questions. You may find it more difficult to write your own questions, but have a go before you have recourse to textbooks. Pay attention to the readability and clarity of your questions, to the layout of the sheet, and to its suitability for the pupils. Take care over drawing any diagrams you include.

Assessment

Repeat the procedure used to assess worksheet A and in particular compare your answers to questions 5-8 with your answers to those questions for worksheet A. Comment briefly below:

1

2

3

4

5

6

7

8

---

9 Was the language used in the questions of the correct level?

10 Did the pupils have any problems of conversion from the language used to the mathematical problem, or of interpreting the answers to the problems in language terms?

11 Were there any difficulties generally experienced by the pupils which suggest the need for further class work?

12 Were there any difficulties experienced by individual pupils which suggest that they might need remedial assistance?

Worksheet C: Introducing a new topic (Week 4)

This is a more ambitious exercise, and if a suitable opportunity does not arise, you may decide to postpone it for a week or two. Here you should try to use the sheet as an instructional medium for new work, so *you will be providing information as well as asking questions.* You will probably find it necessary to use more than one sheet to achieve your aims.

Examples of suitable topics might be recurring decimals, multiplication of 2 X 2 matrices, or reflection. The method can also be used effectively for consolidation or revision, and has obvious advantages with mixed ability classes.

Assessment

Work through questions 1-12 again noting any particular comments below, and paying particular attention to question 5:

Further questions

13 Did you prepare enough work to keep the brightest children occupied for the whole lesson? If not, had you something else up your sleeve?

14 Is this the pupils' normal style of working and if not, what were their reactions to it?

15 Did you have any difficulty with the rigidity of the material in this style of lesson?

16 If you have the opportunity, compare the success (or failure) of your worksheets with that of those commercially produced or produced by other members of staff.

Follow-up

(i) Keep your worksheets carefully for possible future use (for example, place them in manilla folders). When you have a few prepared, devise a suitable filing system.

(ii) Try to remain constructively critical of your worksheets in the future, using the criteria suggested above.

**Focus 4
HANDLING DIFFICULT
CLASSES**

Aim: To help you to come to grips with problems of teaching your more difficult classes.

When to do this: Week 4 (part A) and after half-term, say, Week 6 (part B).

Time to spend: Part A One lesson and preparation and discussion time.
Part B One lesson and discussion time.

What to do: By week 4 of your study period you will start becoming aware of particular difficulties with some of your classes: by now any initial 'honeymoon' period will be over.

A: Coming to grips with a difficult class (Week 4)

(i) *Before the lesson*.

Think of a typical recent incident where discipline has broken down with one or more members of the class and describe it.

Events leading up to the incident:

The incident and the pupils involved:

Your action and its results:

What you would try to do differently if there was a similar incident in future:

Now prepare your lesson even more carefully than usual, making sure you are *thoroughly* familiar with your material and possibly choosing deliberately a teaching topic and method of working you feel happy about. Do not try to change your teaching style or adopt an unfamiliar technique. Make arrangements with a colleague, tutor or fellow-student to observe the lesson *as unobtrusively as possible* and complete the analysis below.

39

(ii) *Analysis*

Date: Class: Topic:

(*To the observer*. The class may behave differently from normal in your presence, but try to keep yourself inconspicuous, use your judgement and make brief notes in the spaces below, concentrating on the points raised.)

1 Lesson beginning

Was the lesson begun promptly and clearly?

Were late comers allowed to spoil this?

Was silence obtained before the teacher spoke?

Was everyone paying attention?

Was the purpose of the lesson made clear?

2 Transitions between activities

Were the changeovers accomplished smoothly?

Was everyone clear about what they were supposed to be doing?

Was there unnecessary noise?

3 Lesson ending

Was there effective summing up or rounding off of the work?

Were any instructions given clearly?

Was the lesson ended promptly?

Was the room left tidy?

4 Preparation

Was the preparation adequate?

Were some (not necessarily all) difficulties anticipated?

Which parts of the preparation (if any) could have been improved?

5 Misbehaviour

What sorts of misbehaviour (trivial, serious or both) occurred?

Describe one incident more fully:

How did the teacher deal with the problem?

Suggest (if you can) how the teacher might deal more effectively with the problem in future:

B: Further attention to discipline problems (After half-term, say week 6)

It is worth taking the opportunity to repeat Part A whenever you are having particular difficulties with a class. Often *a succession of two or three better lessons will boost your morale and restore the class's confidence in you*. A particularly good time to attempt this is immediately after half-term when you are feeling fresher and you will have had more time to think.

You should also work on your management skills which often are the key to successful discipline. To give you some idea of priorities, ask a colleague to watch you teach one of your more difficult classes and then to tick under the nine headings below.

41

(To the observer. After observing the teacher, tick under each of the nine headings below. If possible put three ticks in each of the three columns, high, medium and low. Add any specific comments you may wish to make about class management in the space below the table.)

ASPECT OF CLASS MANAGEMENT	Priority for attention		
	High	Medium	Low
Effective lesson beginnings			
Questions and explanations			
Appropriateness of tasks			
Transitions from one activity to another			
Vigilance and awareness of what is going on			
Response to pupils' work and behaviour			
Teaching manner and relationship with class			
Effective lesson endings			
Preparation of lessons and anticipation of difficulties			

Any other suggestions about improving class management (you may care to look at part A on page 39 before writing this):

You will also wish, of course, to discuss other aspects of the lesson.

Follow-up

(i) Discuss the priorities for attention and the suggestions above with your university or college tutor, and with anyone else who observes your teaching.

(ii) Give special and deliberate attention for the rest of your study period to the high priority points above. Do not, of course, ignore the others.

(iii) You will find further help in this area in: Wragg, E.C., *Class Management and Control*, Basingstoke, Macmillan Education, 1981.

**Focus 5
ORAL QUESTIONING**

Aim: To help you to develop your class questioning skills.

When to do this: Weeks 5 and 7.

Time to spend: Short class teaching periods with various classes up to 15 minutes in length, plus preparation time.

What to do: Mental arithmetic skills are sometimes neglected by modern mathematics teachers. When you know the names of your pupils, you can more easily use short mental arithmetic sessions to help you to develop the skill of distributing questions around the class. Such sessions can be quite brief and used to fill in odd moments at the end of the period, or to sharpen up sluggish minds at the beginning. Arrange to have one such session observed (by a fellow-student, another teacher or a tutor) some time in week 5.

**A: Distributing questions
(Week 5)**

You may prefer to prepare questions in advance until you become more proficient, but you will need a good supply of them (perhaps a hundred or so). Do not just ask straightforward questions like 'Three sevens?', but also ones like 'Three pencils at 7p each?'. 'How many threes in 21?' 'Simplify three twenty-firsts' and so on.

Ensure that there is no shouting out of answers, and do not accept any responses which are made out of turn. It is useful to get pupils to put hands up, but give some questions to those who don't put their hands up. Use names as much as possible at this stage, and do not always accept the first answer given, even if it is correct (though you should later come back with praise for correct responses). Respond gently to incorrect but well-meant answers.

Use your observer to monitor your distribution of questions. Ask him or her to draw a seating plan of the classroom in the rectangle below, and to put a cross on each seat when you ask a question to its occupant.

Examine carefully your distribution of questions. Did you miss any pupils altogether? Did you ask anyone too many questions? Did you pick on girls or boys more? It is important to include every pupil, but you may wish to ask more questions to the weaker members of the class. There are a number of varieties of game where, for example, pupils stand up, and may only sit down on answering a question successfully. These have the danger of exposing the weaker members of the class; and in some forms they give the more able pupils more rather than fewer questions.

If you did not distribute your questions well, try working out a route round the class which takes in everyone, but is apparently random; for example, use a pattern like the multiples of three in a 10 X 10 array of the first hundred digits. You can then repeat the exercise and check if you did any better. If you do use a pattern, then it should be varied from one occasion to another.

B: Developing question skills (Week 7)

This can be done in the same session as A, but is probably better kept for another lesson. Choose a lesson when you want to work with the whole class on the blackboard (or OHP) and you can ask a lot of questions. Suitable topics are properties of quadrilaterals, matrix description of networks and transformation of equations, but there are many others. Again you will need an observer, (who should profit from the session as much as you do) and you should read through the points below and ask the observer to make suitable comments on each of the following common areas of difficulty mentioned. He or she could record your performance under each of the headings with examples of both GOOD and BAD practice.

(i) Vocabulary and clarity

Is the language at the right level and unambiguous at the class's level of understanding? Is any attempt made to tailor the question to the pupil who is being questioned?

(ii) Timing

Does the teacher wait long enough for an answer, or seize too quickly on what the pupil says without giving time for a considered response? Does he or she press too hard for an answer?

(iii) Reinforcement

Does the teacher praise good answers, and develop incomplete or incorrect answers? Are inaudible answers repeated for the whole class to hear, but without sarcasm and exposure to ridicule? Are feelings of rejection in weaker pupils avoided? Are pupils encouraged to use the blackboard when words fail them?

(iv) Prompting

Are pupils who reply 'I don't know' or 'I'm not sure' encouraged to supply more constructive ideas? Does the teacher go back a step or two in the argument or simplify his or her question? Does he or she ask for a second opinion, even when the first is correct? Does he or she genuinely appear to want to know the answer?

Follow-up

(i) Discuss with the observers the skills displayed in the two sessions above and how you can improve them.

(ii) Later in the term tape-record one of your lessons and consider whether you have developed the skills mentioned above.

(iii) Think about the varieties of question you can ask and try to broaden your expertise in this area.

(iv) You will find further help in this area in Kerry, T., *Effective Questioning*, Basingstoke, Macmillan Education, 1982.

Aims: 1 To test in a practical setting the work done in Part 1, Activity 3, and to stress the importance of including such open-ended Activity in pupils' mathematical experiences.
2 To help you to extend the variety of teaching styles you use.

When to do this: Soon after half-term, say weeks 6 and 7.

Time to spend: 2-4 lessons and preparation time.

What to do: In recent years more attention has been paid to open-ended ideas in mathematics teaching, and you will have seen in Activity 3 how mathematics can be developed in an original way from a simple situation. This can help to dispel the feelings of many pupils that mathematics is a cut-and-dried subject where answers are either right or wrong and there is no opportunity for creativity. The use of investigations in the classroom may also help you to extend the range of your teaching techniques.

Read again the work you produced for Activity 3 and decide how you might modify it to suit one of your classes. If it is not suitable, you may decide to investigate another topic (e.g. a combinatorial situation, a simple game or a practical problem), and you will have to do some preliminary work on it. (For students, the class you work with should be one you know fairly well, and you should discuss what you propose to do with the class teacher. In some schools the curriculum is so tightly structured that it may be difficult or impossible for you to try out your investigation, while in others it might be so much a part of the normal work that this Activity is unnecessary. Usually a little tactful negotiation will sort matters out. The success of your investigation will depend not just on your own teaching skills, but also on the pupils' familiarity with this type of work. You may feel in some schools that the work has been relatively unsuccessful when in fact you have been revealing to pupils a completely new view of mathematics which they have not yet had time to absorb fully.)

When you plan the actual lesson, bear in mind the following points:
1 Decide on your teaching method. You may well wish to arrange the pupils in groups or pairs; if so you should decide on the composition of these in advance.
2 Decide, if necessary and possible, how to arrange the classroom furniture in the most appropriate way for your teaching method.
3 Explain the starting point for the investigation carefully, the chief aim being to motivate the pupils to become involved in the Activity.
4 Encourage recording of results (providing suitable materials), pattern recognition and completion, discussion, restrained argument, simple hypotheses and their justification, invention of notation, exploration of blind alleys and fruitful avenues, generalisation and extension of results.
5 This exploration should take at least two periods and if possible some homework time (which may be voluntary).
6 Towards the end of the work develop individual or group recording of discoveries, and writing up of the work or oral explanation of it to the rest of the class.
7 Display any completed work around the classroom where possible.

Title of investigation:

Teaching time proposed:

Brief outline of introductory session:

Materials required:

Assessment of results

1 Record any unexpected mathematical results.

2 Record any comments on pupils' work, especially good work by unexpected pupils or inability to cope with undirected work.

3 Comment on any problems of discipline or classroom management.

4 What are your own reactions to this type of work?

5 Other comments

Follow-up

(i) Make an effort to display pupils' work in an attractive manner. (If you have worked in a primary school, emulate the excellent display work achieved by many primary teachers.)

(ii) If at first you don't succeed . . .

**Focus 7
KEEPING PUPIL
RECORDS**

Aims: 1 To increase your awareness of pupils' individual characteristics.
2 To help you to keep effective records of your pupils' mathematical development.

When to do this: Begin about week 7 of your study period.

Time to spend: Two hours; further time will be needed to update this record and possibly to begin it for other classes which you teach.

What to do: *Confidentiality*. As a teacher you will often have access to private information about pupils and you will write further confidential records yourself. You should ensure that these are seen only by those who have a legitimate reason for doing so. In this Activity you should not, if you are a student, use pupils' names, but should devise some sort of code for yourself. When you keep your own teaching records you should make sure that they are kept private.

Pupil records

Activity 8 introduced you to issues about marking and no doubt you have devised suitable procedures of your own. But marking is only one aspect of keeping pupil records, and while you will find it helpful to keep a neat and tidy mark-book, it is also a good idea to try to extend the scope of your assessment. You will find this particularly helpful in writing meaningful reports on pupils and in coping with interviews on parents' evenings. It may also be valuable in writing references and in dealing with problem pupils. By keeping an explicit record of such progress all these tasks are made easier. There are many ways of keeping such records, and in some schools they are made centrally and kept carefully; but by developing your own system you can tailor it specifically to the needs of mathematics.

Pupil progress sheets

Fill in the pupil progress sheet on page 49 for one of the classes which you know best, preferably a mixed ability class. You can imagine if you like that you are doing this as preliminary preparation for a parents' evening or for writing reports. Use a convenient code to identify the pupils and give their age at some convenient date (often 1 September last). The headings suggest six areas in which you might like to assess your pupils on a five point scale; you may alter these if you wish, and space is added for any categories you might like to add or for additional notes. A small extract showing part of a completed sheet is shown below:

Pupil No. and code	Age (Years and months)	Classroom behaviour	Punctuality and reliability	Neatness and presentation of work	Originality of written work	Response to oral questioning
1 Alan	12.3					
2 Barbara	12.11					
3 Celia	12.1					
4 David	12.6					
5 Elizabeth	12.4					

Pupil No. and code	Age Yrs and mths	Classroom behaviour	Punctuality and reliability	Neatness and presentation of work	Originality of written work	Response to oral questioning	Enthusiasm and enjoyment of subject		
1									
2									
3									
4									
5									
6									
7									
8									
9									
10									
11									
12									
13									
14									
15									
16									
17									
18									
19									
20									
21									
22									
23									
24									
25									
26									

In the example on page 48 six ratings have been made for each pupil on each criterion, one rating for each half term of the academic year. Students will not have time to make as many ratings as this, though you should make a second rating at the end of your teaching practice and compare it with your earlier one. The ratings are made on a five point scale. Each circle placed on the line to the right of a pupil indicates a rating of average on that criterion. If the circle touches the line above or below, this indicates a high or low rating respectively, while if the circle is clear of the line above or below, this indicates a very high or a very low rating. In this way a visual profile of each pupil is quickly available, and much writing and collation of notes avoided.

Alan, for example, is clearly an able mathematician whose classroom behaviour is only average and who needs to take care over the neatness and presentation of his work. Conversely, Barbara emerges as above average on behaviour, punctuality and reliability, and makes efforts to present her work well. Mathematically, however, she is clearly only of average ability. Celia has shown a marked improvement in attitude during the year. Because there is still much scope for further improvement, this might easily have been missed if some less systematic record had been kept. Make similar brief comments about David and Elizabeth in the space below:

David:

Elizabeth:

Consider briefly what other criteria you might use to assess your chosen class, and summarise them briefly in the space below:

Further criteria:

Your record may well highlight particular pupils as being in need of additional help or attention. Pick three such pupils and make some brief suggestions on how you might stimulate them to better work or more socially acceptable behaviour:

Pupil 1

Pupil 2

Pupil 3

Make a mental note of any other pupils to whom you feel you have not given sufficient praise or encouragement and remedy this when you have an opportunity.

Follow-up

(i) Discuss your completed sheet (after you have filled it in) with the class teacher or a colleague. To what extent do you agree or disagree on your assessments?

(ii) Repeat the assessment at the end of your study period. Note any changes, especially in those pupils you singled out for remedial attention.

(iii) Keep your record up-to-date and extend it to other classes.

(iv) Next time you attend a Parents' Evening, assess how much more effectively you deal with parental enquiries.

51

**Focus 8
EXCEPTIONAL PUPILS**

Aim: To encourage you to prepare supplementary teaching material
(a) as a stimulus for able pupils,
(b) as remedial work for less able pupils.

When to do this: Week 8 onwards.

Time to spend: Three hours additional preparation time initially.

What to do: When you begin a new topic with one of your lower school classes observe particularly the reactions of three of your brightest and three of your weakest pupils. It will help if you can choose a mixed ability class, or one with a spread of abilities. You might like to use the results of Focus 7 to help you to choose the pupils. After teaching the class for one or two lessons make brief notes below.

---

1 Has your work challenged the more able pupils? If not, why not?

2 Have the less able pupils been able to follow all you have done? If not, what is the nature of their difficulties?

3 Have any of the pupils caused problems of either a disciplinary or a class-management nature?

Your task is to prepare more suitable materials for the two groups of pupils for the rest of this teaching topic. You can prepare worksheets or workcards or you can find materials in books. You will find it especially useful to use practical materials with the less able pupils. The work should be arranged in such a way that it can be done without undue attention from you. (Remember, in a class of thirty pupils working wholly on task, you have only two minutes in every sixty-minute lesson to spend on each individual child. Administration, whole class in-puts etc. all cut into this small amount of available time.) It need not be exclusive of the work done by the rest of the class; for bright pupils it can be additional work, and for the less able it can be alternative to some of the class work. When the topic has been completed assess the effectiveness of your work.

TOPIC:

For the brighter pupils

Nature of work:

1 Was the additional work relevant to the main class topic?

2 Was the level of the work too hard or too easy?

3 In what ways did it stretch these pupils?

4 What was your reaction to these pupils' performance?

For the weaker pupils

Nature of work:

1 Was the work relevant to the main class topic?

2 Was the level of the work too hard or too easy?

3 Did the tasks help the pupils to overcome learning difficulties?

4 What was your reaction to these pupils' performance?

For both groups

1 In what ways did the additional tasks affect your classroom management problems?

2 In what ways did the work affect the classroom discipline, particularly that of the groups affected?

3 Bearing in mind your answers above, was your additional preparation worthwhile?

4 What changes would you make if you were to repeat this work with a parallel class?

Follow-up

(i) Continue to prepare similar work for this group until the end of your study period and extend it to other classes if possible.

(ii) Talk encouragingly about their work to the children involved and try to obtain some feedback about your special efforts.

(iii) Prepare some enrichment or remedial work as part of your summer term project work or seek advice from specialist colleagues.

(iv) Discuss your work and ideas with fellow students, teachers and tutors.

(v) *Don't neglect the middle-of-the-road pupils.*

(vi) You will find further help in these areas in Bell, P. and Kerry, T., *Teaching Slow Learners*, Basingstoke, Macmillan Education, 1982, and Kerry, T., *Teaching Bright Pupils*, Basingstoke, Macmillan Education, 1981.

Part 3   REFLECTIONS ON EXPERIENCE

For students, the third term sometimes seems an anticlimax after teaching practice. It should be a period of reflection and consolidation, giving you an opportunity to develop some more advanced skills which you will need in your probationary year. You may by this time have obtained your first teaching post, and if so this will give you an opportunity to concentrate your activities in specific directions. Some of the tasks in this part are, therefore, more open in their character, and you should turn this to your own advantage.

You may find that you miss the 'reality' of teaching practice and it is difficult to concentrate on more academic tasks. Most tutors are aware of these problems, but you can do much to overcome them yourself. As a teacher you will be largely independent, so prepare for this now by choosing how you spend your time carefully. It can be very helpful to arrange visits to interesting schools or spend some time each week in school yourself, but it is likely to be you who must take the initiative in arranging these.

More experienced teachers will know that their job requires them to take stock from time to time. A new set of classes, a new school, a new departmental role, will all require the qualified practitioner to re-assess what he or she is doing. For such experienced professionals Activities 13, 15, 16 and 17 can be usefully undertaken as a form of professional renewal. This is particularly important at a time when promotion within the teaching profession is becoming more difficult with falling rolls and a stagnant economy.

Activity	Title	When to do it (for PGCE students)	Date completed
13	Taking stock	Week 1	
14	The method project: Preparation Execution	Weeks 2-6 Weeks 7-8	
15	Assessment of pupils' work	Weeks 2-4	
16	Medium-term planning	Week 5	
17	Goals in mathematics teaching	Week 6	

**Activity 13
TAKING STOCK**

Aim: Now that your classroom-based study period is over, it is a convenient time to assess your strengths and weaknesses in the classroom. You should also be considering in what ways you can equip yourself to develop further the teaching skills considered in Focuses 1-8.

When to do this: During the first week.

Time to spend: One or two hours of your own time, plus formal and informal discussion with colleagues or tutors.

What to do: Consider the classes you have taught recently.

A: The pupils you taught

| Which class did you enjoy teaching most? |
| Year   Ability level |
| Which class did you enjoy teaching least? |
| Year   Ability level |

Try to account for your different feelings about the two classes and the reasons for your different attitudes. Which of the following factors accounted for these feelings?

FACTOR	Very important	Fairly important	Not important
Age of pupils			
Average ability level of pupils			
Range of ability of pupils			
Timing of lessons in day or week			
Rooms you taught in			
Content of syllabus			
The class teacher			
Individual pupil behaviour			
General class attitude			
Others (specify)			

Do your answers say anything about the school in which you worked?

Do your answers say anything about you as a teacher?

B Your methods of teaching Get out your lesson notes for your last full week of teaching and summarise in 5-10 words each of the lessons you taught in that week. Where necessary divide up the lesson by time. For example

Lesson 1: Teacher introduction (20 per cent), pupil exercises (70 per cent), summary (10 per cent).

Lesson 2: Individual work cards.

Lesson 3: Group investigations — finish writing up (50 per cent), group leaders reports (50 per cent).

How much variety of approach do your answers show?

What methods of teaching do you need to find out more about?

What methods are you in danger of overworking?

C Good and bad lessons Find the lesson notes for the most and least successful lessons you have taught in the last three weeks.

Were they with the respective classes you mentioned under A above?

Why was the first lesson such a success? Tick appropriate reasons:

Careful planning	Good pupil behaviour
Interesting subject matter	Good pupil attitudes
Your own enthusiasm (be honest)	Fortunate chance pupil remark
Others (specify)	

What did you put into the lesson which will help to produce such successful lessons in the future?

Why was the second lesson such a failure?

Poor planning	Poor individual behaviour
Depressed teacher performance	Poor class behaviour
Unsupportive class attitudes	Unfortunate incident
Others (specify)	

What circumstances *within your control* would have helped to make this lesson better?

Follow-up

(i) Discuss and compare your answers with colleagues or fellow-students if possible.

(ii) Consider your answers carefully and assess their relevance to your first teaching post, or to your aspirations for future roles or promotion within the profession.

Activity 14
THE METHOD PROJECT

Aim: This is for student teachers, to help you to plan a sustained piece of method work which will
(a) widen your view of mathematics teaching
(b) be useful in your future teaching career.

When to do this: Week 2 to end of term.

Time to spend: Half a day per week for weeks 2-6, about eight days' work in weeks 7 and 8.

What to do: The method project is intended to be your major piece of work in mathematics method during the summer term, and to gain the most benefit from it *you should decide what to do early*. When considering your choice of project you should bear in mind:
(a) If you have already obtained a teaching post, you may wish to do work specifically connected with it. If you have not obtained a teaching post do not use this as an excuse to put off making a decision.
(b) When you are teaching you will find it difficult to make time to carry out a sustained piece of work. You should therefore make the most of this opportunity, which may be the last for some years.
(c) Resources are limited in schools and you may have the opportunity to use ones on your course which you will never meet again. (For example you may be able to make a video-tape.)
(d) You may decide that your experiences last term have shown deficiencies in your knowledge or skills which you would like to remedy.

The range of work which can be done is very large. While your tutor may wish to assess your project work, you should not let this factor influence your choice of project, though of course you should discuss your choice of topic and obtain agreement with him or her. Many teachers are learning to work in teams, and you may agree with other students to work as a small group on a combined project rather than as an individual. The group need not be confined to mathematicians; fruitful groups are often of an inter-disciplinary nature.

Some outlines of possible areas of work, all of which overlap, are:
1 *Collection* of resource materials; for example,
    (a) for domestic or commercial arithmetic: building societies; banking, stocks and shares; bills; hire purchase; income tax; insurance.
    (b) geometrical models
    (c) puzzles, pastimes, fillers and games (Activity 11)
    (d) exercises in various branches of mathematics.
2 *Planning* of future work. Detailed lesson planning is best left until you know your classes better, and you are unlikely to be given the task of designing a complete course in your first year of teaching. However, much planning of a moderately detailed nature may be done at this stage, and may be coupled with the collection of materials above. (See also Activity 16.)
3 *Learning.* You may be painfully aware of gaps in your mathematical knowledge which will have to be covered for your first teaching post. Applications of mathematics in statistics, mechanics and computing often fall into this category. (See also Activity 5.)
4 *Creating.* All projects will be creative to a greater or lesser extent, but the most interesting ones are often those which attempt to prepare more unusual teaching materials; for example,
    (a) Mathematical machines or models such as a harmonograph and other locus generating machines and geometrical models
    (b) Films, filmstrips, tapes, transparencies and other audio-visual aids aimed at developing mathematical awareness.

Outline your own project below:

Note here the resources you will need and set about making sure they will be available:

Follow-up

All the time bear in mind that you should be producing something which will be useful to you in the future.

**Activity 15
ASSESSMENT OF
PUPILS' WORK**

Aims: 1 To aid you in carrying out future assessment of pupils' work.
2 To remind you of the varying reasons for making such an assessment.

When to do this: During weeks 2-4.

Time to spend: About 6 hours.

What to do:
This is a convenient point to remind ourselves of our cognitive objectives in teaching mathematics. In Activity 17 we shall follow this up by thinking in more general terms of the goals of our teaching.

(a) Objectives in mathematics teaching

Bloom's 'Taxonomy' suggests the following main headings for cognitive objectives (Bloom, B.S., Hastings, J.T. and Madaus, G.F., *Handbook on Formative and Summative Evaluation of Student Learning*, New York, McGraw-Hill, 1971). Examples are given in parentheses.

A *Knowledge:*
    (i) of facts and information
        (a) terminology (definitions, symbols)
        (b) specific facts (formulae, relationships)
        (c) conventional methods (classifications, conventions)
        (d) principles and generalisations (theorems)
    (ii) of techniques and skills (computational algorithms, methods of simplification and solution)
B *Comprehension:* the lowest level of understanding
    (a) translation (relationship between graphs and equations)
    (b) interpretation (of graphs, uses of general laws)
    (c) extrapolation, including interpolation (make predictions from graphs, continue a number pattern)
C *Application:* use of general ideas and principles in new situations. Once the application is known it becomes downgraded to A or B.
D *Higher abilities:*
    (a) analysis
    (b) synthesis
    (c) evaluation

(b) Objectives of assessment

The assessment of pupils' work can be of any or all of these objectives. Generally speaking, this assessment becomes more difficult as one descends the list and considers the higher level objectives. Many criticisms of examinations in recent years have, in essence, been that it is precisely these objectives which have not been assessed; and a number of recent attempts have been made to remedy this, for example by asking for teacher assessment of pupils, by including course work in examinations and by asking open-ended examination questions.

In Focus 7 we considered how pupils' progress might be monitored. In this Activity we shall look much more specifically at the marking of pupils' work in tests and examinations. It thus follows on from Part 1, Activity 8. The purposes of examinations vary, and any examination might set out to achieve one or more of the following:

1 measurement of achievement (of cognitive objectives, of psycho-motor skills etc.)
2 selection (for a team, for a job, for university etc.)
3 prognosis (for future success)
4 diagnosis (of faults, of work not done)
5 motivation (in the pre-assessment period)
6 improvement of teaching quality (this, unlike all the above is directed at the teacher).

Consider some of the various examinations and tests you have met in your lifetime (e.g. 'O' and 'A' levels, intelligence tests, driving test, music examinations, team trials at games, oral tests in class and so on). Decide on the objectives of each and elaborate by a few words to make the objectives more specific:

Test/Examination	Objective(s)

Examinations and tests can be set in various ways to achieve the ends noted above, but the three commonest in mathematics examinations at 'O' level and CSE are the longer structured question, the shorter question on a single specific item, and the multiple-choice objective test. The construction of the latter is a skilled task, largely outside the scope of this book; a detailed account is given in Fraser, W.G. and Gillam, J.N., *The Principles of Objective Testing in Mathematics*, London, Heinemann Educational, 1972.

(c) A specification grid

When setting an examination, not only the mathematical objectives A to D considered above should be borne in mind, but also the content of the various questions. It can be helpful to fill in a specification grid. This is easier to do for objective tests since each question then has a more clearly defined aim. Fill in the following specification grid for an examination paper aimed at more able fourth or fifth year pupils; for example, an 'O' level or CSE paper (if possible use a multiple-choice objective test):

Content	A (i)	A (ii)	B	C	D	Total
Arithmetic Algebra Graphical work Geometry Trigonometry Statistics and probability						
Total						

For each question you will have to decide what abilities it tests and in what proportions. For example a traditional geometry question of theorem, proof and rider might have $\frac{1}{3}$ allocated to column A(i) and $\frac{2}{3}$ to column C. You might find very little to place in column D. When you have totalled the rows and columns consider whether their various proportions adequately reflect the content of the syllabus as well as the objectives A-D.

These objectives will now have to be borne in mind when setting up a marking scheme for the examination. The purposes of the examination will also have to be considered; for example, in a school test which will be returned to pupils, it might be desirable to place a greater emphasis on accuracy than would be the case in a public examination where the examiner might wish to reward the correct method of solution more highly, realising that shortage of time is often a reason for the lack of accuracy.

(d) The marking scheme

Great care is taken over the preparation of marking schemes for the traditional type of public examination. The following covers some of the main points allowed for the usual schemes.

1 Marks are labelled M (for method) or A (for accuracy).
2 In most questions about equal weight is given to M and A marks.
3 A marks cannot be given unless the relevant M marks are earned, but M marks do not depend on A marks.
4 Unlabelled marks (or marks labelled with other letters) are given for specific results or statements, and are not dependent on any other marks unless this is stated.
5 The treatment of work crossed out varies with the Board. Usually it is ignored, even if correct; in some boards, however, all work is marked whether crossed out or not; in others, work crossed out is marked only if it is not replaced by other work later.
6 Omission of units is not normally penalised: incorrect units are penalised.
7 Marks are given for steps in the solution which are omitted or implied provided the examiner is satisfied that the candidate has actually solved the question. (Beware cases where the answer is given on the examination paper, and the solution is fudged.)
8 Genuine mis-reading of questions which does not affect the nature or difficulty of the question may be followed through with a loss of 2 or 3 marks (the amount varies in different examinations).
9 If a candidate answers more than the required number of questions, the procedure in most boards is for the questions with the best marks to be counted up to the required number.
10 If a candidate provides two solutions to a question (neither crossed out), that with the higher marks is counted.

The marking scheme is sometimes altered radically at the examiners' meeting, and further co-ordination takes place. In mathematics a great emphasis (perhaps too great) has been placed on consistency of marking between examiners. Discuss the points above with your colleagues or tutor, and decide what alterations you might make to them in the marking of tests and examinations in school (for example, you may not agree with 6).

Exercise

Do this in your department or your mathematics tutorial group. For this exercise each member of your group will require:
(i) Copies of the same four questions of a structured type (i.e. 'long' questions) from an 'O' level paper.
(ii) Two sets of attempted solutions which have been duplicated.
Proceed as follows:
(a) Each member of your group should produce independently a marking scheme for the questions without looking at the attempted solutions.
(b) Each member of your group should mark independently the two sets of attempted solutions.
(c) Compare as a group exercise the marks given for each solution of each question. This is usually a most revealing exercise.
(d) Discuss and agree upon a revised marking scheme to be followed by each member of the group.
(e) Re-mark independently each solution according to the new mark scheme.
(f) Compare the revised marks and try to agree as a group on the final marks awarded.

Follow-up

In the light of your discussions and reflections, re-mark some recent work done for you by your pupils. What changes have you made in your approach to assessing pupils' performance?

**Activity 16
MEDIUM-TERM
PLANNING**

Aim: To extend your planning of teaching to cover the planning of a number of lessons sequentially.

When to do this: About week 5.

Time to spend: Two hours.

What to do: Choose a sequence of topics in teaching which you would expect to cover in six weeks (half a term). If you know what you will be teaching next term, this will be ideal; otherwise you might re-plan lessons for one of the classes you taught last term. The objective is *not* to plan individual lessons in detail but to provide a framework within which individual lessons may be worked out more readily at a later date; about which you can be thinking and reading; and about which you may make some assessment whether you are achieving your overall aims and covering the syllabus with that class. Fill in the following table.

Topic	Week	Content	Style	References	Materials
	1				
	2				
	3				

63

Topic	Week	Content	Style	References	Materials
	4				
	5				
	6				

The table is deliberately restricted in size since it is only necessary to outline what you propose to do. Under individual headings only a word or two should be entered; for example,

Topic: Venn diagrams, linear equations, properties of quadrilateral
Content: Subsets, the function machine, special types of quadrilateral
Style: Worksheets, talk/exercise, test, investigation
References: Texts (use abbreviations) and pages, including exercises
Materials: Graph paper, rulers, prepared worksheets.

You may find it convenient to vary the format slightly. References and materials will help you to prepare duplicated materials in good time, to know where to look for ideas for individual lessons, and to book apparatus which might be required by other teachers. Do not allocate work rigidly to lessons at this stage.

Follow-up

(i) Check how closely you stuck to the table after teaching the topics given.

(ii) Think about the aims and strategies involved in planning over longer periods such as might be done by a head of department.

(iii) What does this exercise tell you about pupils' cognitive and mathematical development over a period of time? How have you ensured progression not just of content but of intellectual demand?

Aim: To examine more closely our goals for the pupils we teach.

When to do this: Week 6.

Time to spend: Two hours.

What to do: Study the following list of goals which is reproduced with permission from the Appendix to the booklet *Evaluation of what, by whom, for what purpose?*, Leicester, Mathematical Association, 1979. (The booklet is obtainable from the Association at the address given on page 71.) You might compare it with the shorter summary of assessment objectives in Activity 15.

PERSONAL SKILLS AND VALUES

The pupil should:

1 read with understanding;
2 communicate verbally, in a precise manner;
3 communicate in writing (words and symbols) in a precise manner;
4 think clearly and precisely; reason both inductively and deductively;
5 think flexibly and approach new situations with confidence;
6 be able to organise his own work and learning, i.e. have learned how to learn;
7 be creative — able to pose his own questions, invent his own methods and symbols etc., and be able to use imagination;
8 be able to weigh evidence and be prepared to change his point of view according to this evidence;
9 be able to appreciate cultures other than his own, and be interested in the world and other people.

MATHEMATICAL KNOWLEDGE AND INTELLECTUAL SKILLS

The pupil should

10 acquire an understanding of the fundamental number relationships;
11 know and implement laws of mathematical operations;
12 develop a familiarity with normal mathematical procedures, based on an understanding of their development;
13 relate mathematical techniques to everyday life and apply certain concepts and skills in realistic problems and investigations;
14 recognise mathematical concepts and have a knowledge of the criteria related to those concepts;
15 appreciate the normal algorithmic processes and use them with understanding in the solution of problems;
16 use appropriate language in recognition, description and classification; use the symbols and notation of mathematics to show it is a language with rules and a vocabulary;
17 develop the ability to interpret mathematical data in a variety of forms; recognise patterns and relationships; be able to generalise from experience;
18 relate mathematics to other disciplines in the curriculum;
19 develop the ability to apply mathematical principles to new situations;
20 acquire skill in distinguishing facts and establishing their inter-relationships;
21 develop the ability logically to order and process facts to lead to the solution of problems;

22 develop logical thinking through the study of mathematics;
23 develop the ability to collect original data;
24 acquire skill in applying appropriate criteria to original data in order to organise and evaluate the material, and to draw conclusions;
25 develop the intellectual skills necessary to suggest hypotheses based on original data;
26 understand the idea of a mathematical model;
27 recognise the unified structure of the subject and integrate the separate branches when solving problems or carrying out investigations.

MATHEMATICAL APPRECIATION
The pupil should:
28 enjoy and be interested in mathematics and have a good attitude towards the subject;
29 have confidence and resourcefulness when working at mathematics;
30 work with enthusiasm, determination and concentration on the subject and be well motivated to continue;
31 develop a willingness to participate, and exhibit interest in mathematics;
32 develop creative and imaginative attitudes towards mathematics;
33 acquire appreciation of mathematical criteria;
34 gain intellectual stimulus from the study of mathematics;
35 derive satisfaction from achieving conclusions to mathematical processes;
36 acquire the commitment necessary to initiate original work;
37 develop the confidence to analyse and evaluate new data;
38 see the subject as relevant and useful to everyday experience, and appreciate the value and contribution of mathematics to society;
39 experience excitement and intellectual satisfaction through mathematics;
40 develop an attitude of critical awareness;
41 develop a conviction in the general validity of mathematics.

GENERAL AND PHYSICAL SKILLS
The pupil should:
42 know about the contributions of some leading mathematicians and the historical development of some mathematical concepts, e.g. measurement of time, the calendar;
43 abstract general principles, based on experiences with concrete materials;
44 be aware of some modern applications, e.g. linear programming, operational research;
45 develop physical skills in the use of mathematical instruments;
46 develop the physical control to make precise drawings;
47 co-ordinate physical and intellectual skills when solving problems or carrying out investigations.

In this Activity you are asked to analyse the goals which are implicit in some of your teaching. This is not an easy task, but it is worth doing, for it will help you to widen your view of your teaching, and may assist you to pinpoint areas in which it is deficient. Usually goals such as those above are accepted unconsciously and teachers do not deliberately try to design lessons to fulfil them; it is salutary to ask oneself from time to time what one expects pupils to achieve.

Choose two successful but contrasting lessons you have taught recently and describe them in detail below. Use your lesson notes, but expand them where necessary. In the right hand column note the numbers of the goals which were covered by each part of the lesson. Some examples are given in the booklet *Why, What and How?*, Leicester, Mathematical Association, 1976, which also repeats the list of goals given above.

LESSON 1   Title: Age group: Ability:

Details of lesson	Goals (give numbers)

LESSON 2   Title: Age group: Ability:

Details of lesson	Goals (give numbers)

Look through the list of goals again and note below those which you did not attempt to achieve in your lessons.

```


```

Could any of these goals have appropriately been achieved in either lesson? Give brief details:

```


```

On which goals do you think you should place more emphasis in your future teaching?

```


```

Discuss the list of goals with your colleagues or fellow-students, and make further notes below:

Name any goals in the list which you think are inappropriate:

Have you any other goals which you think ought to be included in the list?

Follow-up

Repeat the above exercise (formally or informally) from time to time throughout your teaching career.

THE PROBATIONARY YEAR: A Postscript for Student Teachers

The word probation is, perhaps, unfortunate but there is no doubt that many experienced teachers look back on their first year of teaching as the most difficult of their career. The chief aim of this book has been to help you to improve your own teaching of mathematics. From now on you will be almost entirely responsible for this. Most teachers can count on the fingers of one (often mutilated) hand the number of visits they have had from inspectors and advisers, not because these people do not wish to help, but because they have not the time to do so. Heads of department, too, are often so busy that you might be reluctant to ask them to spare time to watch you teach.

Like all other probationary teachers you will have problems, but you will soon learn to overcome them. There is not sufficient space in this booklet to give detailed tasks here as in the first three parts, and in any case the diverging needs of different teachers make that difficult. Many of the tasks given earlier in the booklet can, however, be repeated with great benefit, and the 'follow-ups' will suggest more ideas. Other problems cannot easily be dealt with in this type of format and you will need to seek help elsewhere.

A small survey of mathematics teachers in their first three years of teaching showed that the four commonest problems in their order of importance are:

1 Discipline

Some children are difficult to control under any circumstances, so do not expect instant success. Admit your problems and be prepared to talk about them to other teachers. You may be able to get help from your head of department or your mathematics adviser, but often it is easier to talk to younger teachers who are only just solving their own problems. Try to see other teachers· at work, not only in your own subject but in others and especially with the classes you teach. In return try to get them to watch and criticise you. Even though they are often harsher than tutors and advisers in their criticism, it is easier to take because they are your peers.

Try to sort out how you will deal with the more obvious problems beforehand.·Know what punishments you will hand out for bad work, work not done, rudeness, aggression, breaking school rules. Keep a record of punishment given and make sure it is completed. Deal with problems yourself if you can, but learn where to take the ones you can't cope with yourself. Do not be soft-hearted, especially at first; curiously, your pupils will not respect you for it. On the other hand, get to know your pupils as people, and try to understand them. Look again at Activity 10 and Focus 4. Above all, do not be so obsessed by discipline that you stifle your own teaching.

2 Teaching the less able and remedial teaching

Simplicity and flexibility are key words with the less able. The hardest problem is to engineer success for your pupils; it is no good repeating old failures; and they must perceive the success for themselves. You will need to spend more time in preparation and less in marking. Remember Activity 9 when preparing work, as well as Focuses 4 and 8, and Activity 16. Teachers find it easier to admit their failures with the less able so it will be easier to discuss your problems with others. Accept ideas with humility, even from non-mathematics teachers. Vary the work, one successful course for the less able has one double period per week on a project (e.g. transport, salaries, football league tables) each lasting half a term, one double period doing worksheets on simplified ideas from the CSE syllabus, and single periods on number work and mathematical games. Do not be too ambitious in the amount of preparation – teachers with nervous breakdowns do not help their pupils. A useful list of suitable teaching materials may be found in *Mathematics in School*, Volume 9, No. 3, May 1980.

Remedial teaching is a specialist task in one sense, and outside the scope of this booklet. Remedial teachers have a particular camaraderie and you will get much help from them if you ask. You will also face remedial tasks within the classes you teach – often these are due to absence of pupils causing them to omit vital work. Here is an opportunity for you to demonstrate your particular care and concern for individual pupils.

3 School organisation and pastoral care

It is surprising that many young teachers find it difficult to follow school organisation. You should find out as much as you can as early as you can: it is embarrassing to admit that you do not know at any time, but easier when you are a newcomer. Part of the problem is sometimes keeping track of all the pieces of paper coming your way, so put them tidily in some sort of file.

Pastoral care is part of your responsibility as a teacher. Try to get to know your pupils quickly (Focus 1). You may find it helpful to keep notes on individuals for yourself. If you do this, be careful about what you write and keep it confidential.

4 Diagnosis of pupils' difficulties

This is an area which takes time to master. Two useful articles are those by Alistair McIntosh in *Mathematics Teaching* nos. 83 and 87 (June 1978 and June 1979). While these are about top junior school children, they give some idea of the care needed in analysis of individual problems.

Activities 8 and 15 will help you with marking, but the diagnosis of difficulties is a little more intimate than the tasks implied there; and this reminds us again of the need for individual help for many pupils. Teaching is not just talking to a whole class, but also includes much individual contact, and this is often more fruitful in the long run.

TIME

Most young teachers find that the root cause of many of their problems is time. First, they lack time to perform all the tasks needed to carry out their job well, and second, they need time to develop their skills. Careful organisation is the biggest help with the first aspect of the problem. It is a good idea to try to get all your marking done at school so that you do not have to carry piles of books and papers home. Be careful to keep up to date with your marking; it is fatal to let it get out of hand, but do not allow marking to take precedence over lesson preparation.

The second aspect of time is simply that you will need several years to develop your teaching skills; good teachers, like good wine, need time to mature. When you look back at some of your 'early failures' you will cringe at them, but you will find that you will improve very rapidly in the first three or four years, even though the improvement may not be perceptible to you at the time.

PROFESSIONALISM: A FINAL THOUGHT

Teachers, tutors and heads are all professionals; teaching is much maligned at times but still a profession. You can help to raise the status of the teaching body as a whole if you accept this. One aspect of professionalism is the acceptance by the individual of the need for personal growth and development in his or her career. This can be done by reading books and journals, by meeting other teachers in your own and other schools for discussion, by developing schemes of work as a group activity and by attending in-service courses. If you belong to one (or both) of the two mathematics teaching associations you will find this a great help in keeping you up to date. Their addresses are below, and while you are a mathematics teacher, the subscriptions are tax deductible.

The Mathematical Association
259 London Road,
LEICESTER. LE2 3BE

The Association of Teachers of Mathematics,
Kings Chambers,
Queen Street,
DERBY. DE1 3DA

Both subscriptions include a journal — respectively *Mathematics in School* and *Mathematics Teaching* — and regular reading of these can provide you with new ideas to keep your teaching fresh. Both also publish various reports and many other booklets about teaching which are invaluable in the classroom. For students an inexpensive booklet which you will find particularly useful is *Starting as a Mathematics Teacher* published by the Mathematical Association (1981). You will also find it helpful to build up a small library of useful books; a few which I find particularly helpful on the teaching of mathematics are given on page 72.

Finally, best wishes in your teaching career.

FURTHER READING

Banwell, C., Saunders, K.D. and Tahta, D., 1972, *Starting Points for Teaching Mathematics in Middle and Secondary Schools*, O.U.P., London. (Invaluable for open-ended work but unfortunately out of print).

Brissenden, T.H.F., 1980, *Mathematics Teaching: Theory in Practice*, Harper and Row, London. (Up-to-date, particularly helpful on lesson planning and teaching style.)

Cockcroft, W.H. (Chairman), 1982, *Mathematics Counts*, Report of the Committee of Inquiry into the Teaching of Mathematics in Schools, H.M.S.O., London. (Sets the scene for the present day, remarkably readable for a government report.)

Cornelius, M.L. (ed.), 1982, *Teaching Mathematics*, Croom Helm, London. (Raises problems and sets perspectives — complements the Cockcroft Report well.)

Hart, K.M. (ed.), 1981, *Children's Understanding of Mathematics: 11-16*, John Murray, London. (An important piece of recent research with real classroom applicability. Some very worrying conclusions about teaching.)

Mathematics Curriculum Series, 1977-8, Six Books: *Number, Counting and Configurations, Algebra, Geometry, From Graphs to Calculus, Mathematics across the Curriculum,* Blackie, Glasgow. (Fundamental for teaching aspects of the mathematics curriculum in the 11-16 age range.)

Polya, G., 1957, *How to Solve it*, Princeton University Press. (Invaluable for ideas on problem-solving, a classic.)

Skemp, R.R., 1971, *The Psychology of Learning Mathematics*, Penguin. (Needs up-dating, but still the most readable in its field.)